THE CLIENT STAMPEDE

7 SIMPLE STEPS

THE CLIENT STAMPEDE

GET MORE CLIENTS,
MAKE MORE MONEY,
HAVE MORE FUN.

JULIE GUEST

Published by Blue Sky Publishing, New York, NY

BLUE SKY
Publishing

www.BlueSkyPublisher.com

The Client Stampede is available at special discounts for bulk purchases for sales and marketing promotions or corporate use. Special editions including personalized covers, or an excerpt of the book with corporate logos, can be created in large quantities for customized needs. For more information please contact Premium Sales hello@blueskypublisher.com

Library of Congress Cataloging-in-Publication Data is available upon request.

Guest, Julie

ISBN   9780578897554
eBook ISBN   9780578897561

Proudly printed in the United States of America.

Second Edition.

Cover design by Bolder&Louder – Extraordinary Advertising. Ingenious Strategy.
www.BolderLouder.com

"Don't bunt.
Aim out of the
ballpark. Aim for
the company of
immortals."

DAVID OGILVY

"Average will not be my legacy."

KOBE BRYANT

This book is dedicated to my daughter, my North Star, and to all our private clients and coaching students. It is an honor to be a part of your growth.

I also dedicate this book to you—the reader. A world of infinite possibility is about to open up, and I am excited to take you on this journey.

THANK YOU FOR HELPING

20% of all author royalties are donated to some of my favorite charities including SmileTrain, Meals on Wheels, Heifer International, International Rescue Committee and various local animal shelters like the Rottweiler Rescue of Los Angeles, and the Ann Arbor and Louisiana Humane Societies.

CONTENTS

Hello Hare 1

The Promise and Why You Need to Read This Book 9

My Story: Saved by the Client Stampede Formula™ 13

Detoxing from Marketing Myths 21

THE 7-STEP CLIENT STAMPEDE FORMULA

STEP 1. Target Market—The WHO 31

STEP 2. Irresistible Messaging. Forget Smoke Signals, Bring In
The Freight Train 47

STEP 3. Power Branding & Celebrity Positioning 67

STEP 4. Packaging It Up 93

STEP 5. Price, Price, Baby, and Sales Ascension 99

STEP 6. Your High Performance Marketing Engine 109

STEP 7. Creating Extraordinary Experience 141

(Not) Final Words 145

Common Marketing Problems and Their Solutions 149

About Julie Guest 155

Acknowledgments 159

One Ask 164

Hello Hare

*"The only impossible journey is
the one that never begins."*

TONY ROBINSON

Welcome to a much better, more fun way to run your business.

Owning a successful business is not for the faint of heart. You already know this (and have the battle scars to prove it). But you also know there's a hard way and an easy way to do everything.

What's the hard way? Learning by trial and error.

What's the easy way? Finding someone who's already walked that path and learn everything you can from them.

I'm honored to be your guide for this journey. You'll find me blunt, sometimes annoyingly honest, *but I'll also be your biggest cheerleader.*

I know your business is capable of great things—things greater than you've probably ever imagined. Frankly, the world needs you and your business to succeed in a huge way. Why? Because well-run, ethically-led businesses that deliver real value to their clients, are rare.

I *know* you've got what it takes.

The fact that you've reached this stage in your business journey and are actively seeking ways to improve and grow, shows you're already someone who moves quickly, while others are still waiting for the perfect conditions so they can make their move.

You have your sights set on big goals, you're decisive, you're impatient (you wanted results *yesterday*), and you often move at speeds that make people's heads spin. Which makes me think you just might be a hare, like me.

They Got the Story All Wrong

Remember the story of the hare and the tortoise? You know the one where the tortoise wins because "slow and steady" wins the race? In business I have found the opposite to be true. The tortoises of the business world wander about at a leisurely pace, "waiting" for things to get better.

They tuck their heads into their shells when the going gets tough and pretend change is not happening. They keep marketing their businesses the same old way they've always done it, getting frustrated with results but not being willing to take out their wallets to invest in solutions that will help them.

Occasionally, a tortoise will look sideways to see what the other tortoises are doing. Sometimes they'll copy them, thinking they must know better. But they rarely, if ever, do.

Tortoises complain a *lot*. There's always a reason (usually someone else's fault) why their business is struggling. They typically have grand ideas, but just don't execute them. They prefer to "play it safe," and avoid making decisions in case they make a "wrong one."

As you may have already guessed, tortoises are not known for their innovation. They don't lead. They're most comfortable when they're following. (Or wishing things would just go back to the way they were—the good old days.)

Meanwhile, the hare, the *real* hero of the story, is very busy *not* following other tortoises. After all, life's too short to sit around waiting for things to happen. The hare always has a game plan, is always taking action, and is always looking for the fastest route to get to his destination.

Sometimes this means the hare's path looks like this:

But as the hare well knows, the riskiest strategy of all is not taking a risk. He knows that, and that in order to win, you have to sometimes take imperfect action and pivot on the run.

While the tortoise is patiently waiting for the perfect plan and the perfect time, slowly just putting one foot in front of the other, the impatient hare has already lapped the course ten times, recruited other hares to run the course on his behalf, licensed the business model and retired to a desert island filled with carrots. Sadly, in some instances the tortoise never actually reaches the finish line. This is because he took so darn long that the course completely changed ... and he lost his way.

A Business Blueprint for Hares

Executing the Client Stampede Formula™ in your business is like giving the hare the blueprint to the course, complete with all the shortcuts, pitfalls to watch out for, new and bigger ideas to monetize the business model and an earpiece with step by step navigation.

I discovered the Client Stampede Formula™—a time-proven, in-the-trenches, battle-tested method of attracting all the business you need in any economy—by accident. In the worst economic downturn in over a century.

It was a life-saver for me, and it got me out of an impossibly tight spot. It's also been the most transformative process I've used to grow our clients' businesses over the years.

Why is this?

Because the Formula leapfrogs results and accelerates success no matter how cut-throat an industry is, or how price-competitive, or even how bad the overall economy is.

BUT KNOW THIS.

The Client Stampede Formula™ is not a magic silver bullet. It takes an open mind, a dose of humor, laser-like focus, and action, in order for it to work. But it *is* a simple, 7-Step process that can be followed by anyone, in any sized business, in any industry, anywhere in the world.

There are many people who profit enormously from the complexity of and confusion surrounding marketing. I am not one of them.

The Client Stampede Formula™ cuts through the BS and will enable you to assess, with razor-sharp precision, if a marketing opportunity makes sense for your business *or not.* You'll be able to clearly articulate why your business is the best, and you'll know how to craft offers so irresistible that your target market will come running and your competitors will wonder how on earth you did it…

You'll never get sucked into marketing hype again or waste your marketing budget chasing shiny marketing tools. Imagine instead, a waiting-list business offering the most innovative and highest margin products and services of anyone in its industry. Your marketing headaches will be a thing of the past.

You'll understand the power of a marketing engine, and how it can run essentially on autopilot, working as your unpaid sales force, to attract, sort, and convert your leads while you sleep soundly at night. Finally, you'll be the one in control of the number of new clients you attract every day and the rate at which your business grows. You, not outside factors.

I know what you're thinking. "This all sounds great but will it work on my business?" The answer is yes. To date, I've used the Client Stampede Formula™ directly on 300+ businesses in 72 different industries (and counting). I've also helped over 50,000 businesses apply it through my programs and trainings.

The businesses I've helped span a huge range of industries, from real estate and financial services, manufacturing, alternative energy, and hospitality, to beauty and fashion, information marketing, education, health care, technology, publishing, marketing, and advertising...from tiny brands to global luxury ones. Upmarket, down market. Big city, small town. Start-up business, Fortune 100. You get the idea.

This simple 7-Step formula *will* work for your business.

We just covered a lot of ground. Let's recap:

1.   It doesn't matter how big or how small your business is.

2.   It doesn't matter what kind of marketing tactics you have (or haven't) done in the past.

3.   3. It doesn't matter what marketing strategies have (or haven't) worked for you in the past.

4.   It doesn't matter whether your marketing department is one thousand people or just you (an army of one).

5.   It doesn't matter what industry you are in.

6.   It doesn't matter how price-sensitive your industry is.

7.   It doesn't matter how fiercely competitive your industry is.

8.   It doesn't matter what the economy is doing—booming or recession.

None of these things are relevant to your success. All that matters is that you apply the formula.

Now I'm going to be annoyingly honest. This book is NOT for you if:

1. You were nodding your head in agreement when I was talking about some of the tortoise's habits. That's ok. Not everyone is cut out to be a hare.

2. Innovation is not your thing. You're comfortable staying in your comfort zone—status quo baby! The idea of doing things differently (sometimes radically differently), and embracing change to thrive, makes you break out in hives.

3. You're what I call "marketing jaded" ("MJ"). I can usually identify an MJ a mile away because here's what I typically hear them say: "But we've already tried that, and it didn't work!" (Insert whiny tone.) If you're an MJ, that's ok. *Most people are.* But we can't be friends. *Just because you tried something and it didn't work doesn't mean that it doesn't work. It just means that YOU couldn't get it to work.*

4. Your business is not based on a strong ethical foundation, meaning either you're selling things you don't actually believe in, or you're engaged in some illegal activity. In other words, your business does NOT make the world a better place. For example, if you're a financial advisor selling products or investments that you would never personally invest your own money in, then this book is not for you. Or, if your business is in the tobacco, gambling or porn industry, it's not for you either.

If any of these attributes describe you, please return this book from wherever you purchased it and ask for your money back. The Client Stampede Formula™ is not for you.

You're still with me? Great! I *knew* you would be.

Let's get rolling.

IF YOU'RE IN A BIG HURRY
SKIP TO PAGE 156.
IF YOU'VE GOT TIME,
TURN THE PAGE AND
LET'S DIVE IN.

The Promise and Why You Need This Book

"If you obey all the rules, you miss all the fun."

AUDREY HEPBURN

When you implement the Client Stampede Formula™ in your business, you'll be able to:

1. Innovate faster and more strategically, knowing ahead of launch if you have a slam-dunk winner or not.

2. Cherry-pick the best prospects in your market.

3. Quickly and easily identify new target markets to enter, and determine quickly and cost-effectively if they will be profitable—or not.

4. Separate yourself from your competitors once and for all— never be confused with them again.

5. Never again compete on price.

6. Double, even triple your prices, and now you have the right marketing message, have your customers happily pay them.

7. Be in control of cash flow. No more feast or famine peaks and troughs. Slow periods will be a thing of the past because you'll know how to create new business on demand.

8. No more Frankenstein marketing—that means looking and sounding schizophrenic across different media forms because your branding isn't cohesive. Instead, allow your consistency to build trust with customers like never before.

9. Stop wasting marketing budget on useless advertising that doesn't work. Your Marketing ROI will skyrocket. All guesswork about whether your marketing is working will be eliminated.

10. Easily identify whether a new media to advertise on is an excellent fit for your company or not, and how to test it quickly.

11. Replace your headache clients with new, highly appreciative clients who will happily pay you more.

12. Attract more of your best clients.

13. Have more fun with your marketing.

14. Stop chasing shiny marketing objects.

15. Bombproof your business to thrive through the next recession, global virus, or act of political stupidity.

16. Transform your industry through your innovation.

17. Attract and keep the best talent who'll scramble to work for you.

18. Quadruple+ the size of your sales force without recruiting more people.

19. Increase your profit per customer.

20. Have happier, more engaged employees, including an ecstatic salesforce.

21. Accelerate revenue growth rate.

22. Significantly increase revenue per employee.

Now that we've covered the power of the Client Stampede Formula™ and what it can do for your business, let's sit down so I can share my embarrassing story about a terrible decision I made, and how my discovery of the Formula saved me.

"Everything negative - pressure, challenges - is all an opportunity for me to rise."

KOBE BRYANT

Saved by the Client Stampede Formula

"If opportunity doesn't knock, build a door."

MILTON BERLE

don't know what you were doing during the last recession, but I was busy digging myself out of a very deep hole of my own making. It was February 2008. As you'll recall, the housing bubble had imploded in spectacular fashion, and the global recession was in full swing. I was living in Los Angeles at the time, and less than two years earlier, had managed to purchase a house at the very peak of the market, proudly beating out five other offers and paying above asking price.

In my defense, I had been house-hunting for six months and had lost out on nine other houses. This one, I was determined not to lose. It was a 1483 sq. ft, three bed, two bath ranch house built in 1953 on an oversized postage stamp. There was no backyard to speak of—just a pool. The neighbors could look in on all three sides. The kitchen had the original blue and white swirled Formica countertops and no dishwasher. The bathrooms? Think lovely white tiles, stained yellow over the years with full wall mirrors edged with black spots from the moisture.

What the house did have going for it was good bones, including original hardwood floors and a floor-to-ceiling natural stone fireplace (which, sadly, I had no reason to use as this was, after all, Los Angeles). It was also in a decent location in the South Bay, in an okay school district. But otherwise, it was an unremarkable house.

The price I paid for this retro shoebox? $640,000. And, as you may have already guessed, I took full advantage of the generous financing on offer at the time and took out the biggest loan the bank would allow—95%.

Unfortunately, buying at the peak of the market and leveraging myself to the hilt weren't the only mistakes I made; there was one more. This one was particularly memorable.

I was so eager to beat out the other buyers I unconsciously skipped an essential step of due diligence.

At the end of the road was a 10ft high brick wall painted white. You would think surely I would have peeked over the other side to see what was behind it. Nope. Didn't happen. Well, it *did* happen when I was taking my dog for the first walk after closing, but by then, it was too late.

Behind the big white wall, in true Los Angeles fashion, was a mobile home park. But not the tidy, well-kept kind. This one sat at the far opposite end of the spectrum. There were beer bottles and broken glass strewn about, windows frames with glass either missing or hanging by a corner, piles of trash wedged under makeshift entryways, abandoned cars with flat tires... oh, and the smell! I felt like I had walked into some kind of apocalyptic movie scene.

Fast forward to Christmas 2007. The economy had tanked. Property values in our neighborhood and all over Los Angeles were dropping like stones. We were in a pickle. My husband at the time had just been offered a job in Arizona flying commercial helicopters, and we needed to move. By this time, I had been running my own marketing agency for about 18 months. I had been lucky enough to secure a few good-sized contracts, including one with a Fortune 100 company, and even though my team was based in Los Angeles, relocating to Arizona and working remotely wouldn't be a problem.

The problem was we were upside down on our house.

Real estate agents were fleeing their industry like rats on a sinking ship. The few brave souls who remained only picked the low-hanging fruit to sell, and after hearing how much we owed, no agent wanted to touch our house with a barge pole.

Someone wise once said that necessity is the mother of all invention. I have found this to be particularly true at many times in my life. Especially at this one. With no other option (aside from giving the house back to the bank, which was not an option), I rolled up my sleeves. If there was ever a time to test my marketing chops, it was now.

I knew that whatever we did next had to be so completely different from anything else in the real estate industry, that people would be stopped in their tracks.

I also knew I had to design a process people could follow—a sales process for people to follow so that the houses didn't just grab attention, but actually got sold.

I knew I had to be **very strategic** because I needed to squeeze every possible dollar out of the house's value. I did not want to be going to the closing table with my checkbook.

So Here's What I Did

I created a marketing campaign that would run for seven days only. It would launch on a Monday morning and finish at 5pm the following Sunday evening. My plan was to light up our neighborhood and all the surrounding areas with our advertising. The goal? To drive as many people as possible to our two-day open house on Saturday and Sunday. The house would be sold on Sunday evening at 8pm to the highest bidder.

To put things in perspective, at that time a real estate agent considered an open house a *big success* if three groups of people came through on a weekend.

Here's What Happened

We launched our marketing campaign on Monday as planned, but as word started to spread, *all hell broke loose*. Our phone rang all hours of the day and night, and we had people peeking in our windows and knocking on our front door, begging to get a sneak preview before the weekend open house.

We also had three different real estate agents show up, two accusing us of selling our house illegally (i.e., without the help of an agent, which is total baloney), and an enlightened one asking if her company could hire us to do their marketing.

When Saturday 10am finally arrived and we opened our front door, there were about thirty people lined up outside waiting to get in.

By the time the weekend open house was over, we were exhausted. We'd had well over 200 people through the door and, most importantly, **we were able to sell the house to the highest bidder for $2,000 more than we owed.**

What was most interesting to me as a marketer was that **the lucky buyers weren't even looking for a house to buy.** They lived a few blocks down the street, saw our advertising, and, like most people, stopped in out of curiosity to see what was going on. They ended up falling in love with the house and buying it for their daughter, so she could live closer to them.

The process I followed, of essentially creating demand out of thin air irrespective of what the economy is doing, taught me many valuable marketing lessons that have become the cornerstone of our marketing agency:

1. **Ignore what anyone else is doing or saying.** Ignore what the economy is doing. Be like a horse with blinders on. If you have the right message matched to the right market, you can create demand out of thin air. Great marketing creates its own demand!

2. **Don't wait for the tide to turn.** Create your own client stampede. Create your own opportunity.

3. **Different always wins.** In the game to grab eyeballs when competition is at fever pitch, the worst thing you can do is have boring advertising. Or copy your competitors. If we had copied other real estate agents' advertising (a contender for the worst advertising of possibly any industry), my life would have taken a very different trajectory, and I would

possibly still own a certain house in LA with trailer park neighbors...

4. **Change the game – don't follow the rules.** I knew we could only get top dollar for the house if there was fierce competition for it. By changing up the process—the way in which the house would be sold—I got to make the rules and tip the odds in our favor. Don't get me wrong. This wasn't about taking advantage of our buyer or trying to short-change them in any way. It was the absolute opposite. Our buyers were *thrilled* to be able to buy the house because they had beaten out the other 20+ other offers, *and* their daughter got to live in a great home, in walking distance from their own. They just didn't know they wanted to buy a house until they saw our marketing and walked into ours. **By creating our process, we then controlled the process.** We attracted as many people as possible, to attract as many offers as possible, to sell the house to the person who wanted it the most.

5. **Putting a high-performance marketing system in place was the secret to our success.** To ensure that no lead was wasted and we had the highest chance of conversion (getting an offer), I left nothing to chance. I systemized every aspect of our marketing, from the way we advertised, to the voice message left on our phone, the script we used to walk people through the house, to the handouts they were given. Nothing was done 'seat-of-the-pants'. Every piece of our system worked together and the experience was delivered as consistently as possible to maximize response rates and conversion. (More about this in Chapter 6: Building Your Marketing Engine.)

This methodology of creating overwhelming demand, no matter the circumstances, is what I call the Client Stampede Formula™.

And it's based on the seven simple steps I'm about to take you through.

I'm excited to share the formula. But before we dive in, we need to detox your mind of any preconceived ideas about what great marketing *is* and *isn't*, so you can clear any noise in your head and begin with a clean slate.

"If you always put a limit on everything you do, physical or anything else, it will spread into your work and into your life. There are no limits. There are only plateaus, and you must not stay there, you must go beyond them."

BRUCE LEE

Detoxing from Marketing Myths

"Half the money I spend on advertising is wasted; the trouble is I don't know which half."

JOHN WANAMAKER

I estimate at least 96% of all advertising spend is 100% wasted. This is based on my in-the-trenches experience working with hundreds of companies worldwide, and as a consultant doing in-depth marketing audits for large companies as part of their transformation marketing.

It's time to hit the reset button. As an industry, marketing and advertising takes the cake for using the most smoke and mirrors, being confusing beyond belief, and for perpetuating misinformation. This, in turn, results in massive amounts of wasted advertising spend.

According to the research company, Statistica, in 2020, advertising spend in the USA, including digital (desktop/laptop and mobile), directories, magazines, newspapers, out-of-home, radio, and TV, was $263 billion. Based on my estimates, this means a staggering $252 billion every year is wasted marketing spend. You may as well set fire to a Mount Olympus-sized pile of money.

Why is so much money wasted?

Primarily, because of belief in some or all of these myths:

1. Everyone is our customer
2. Digital advertising rules. All other advertising, dead
3. Brand, brand, brand. We must only advertise our brand
4. If it works for them, it will work for us
5. Marketing and advertising are the same thing

Let's set the record straight.

1. Everyone Is NOT Your Customer

"If they've got a pulse, they're our customer" is the war-cry of mediocre businesses everywhere. There's no faster way to decimate your marketing ROI than by spreading your marketing dollars thinly over as many different markets as possible. As incredible as your business is, you can't be all things to all people. And you don't want to be.

The greatest margins lie in being specialists, not generalists. Just think of the difference between what it costs to see your family doctor for a checkup, versus an appointment with a heart surgeon. Being a specialist to a much smaller target market (or markets— who said you have to only confine yourself to one?) is far more lucrative, with much less competition, and will fast track your company's growth. (See Step 1 of the Client Stampede Formula™ for more on this.)

2. Digital Advertising Is Wonderful, but It Is NOT the Be-All and End-All of Marketing.

Zig when others zag. Extraordinary opportunities lie in overlooked media which your competition has abandoned.

I love digital marketing. In five minutes, we can create an ad, run it and know within fifteen minutes if it's a winner or not. For our clients, digital marketing is a critical component of their marketing system (see Step 6 of the Client Stampede Formula™). We run hundreds of thousands of digital ads for our clients' marketing engines every month. We also optimize their online profiles, and blog, tweet, post, respond to prospect queries,,, you know the drill.

Digital ads can be run for pennies on the dollar. BUT… millions of people and their grandmas are also running digital marketing campaigns, and are blogging, tweeting, videoing, and posting up a storm. The online noise is insane. **We are being assaulted with the worst kinds of online advertising all day, every day, making it harder than ever to attract the attention of the best prospective buyers.** This is why the vast majority of digital marketing is so wasteful.

Turning up the volume on your online advertising (i.e., running a greater volume of the same kind of ads) isn't going to give your business a breakthrough. And remember, your competitor's storefront is just one click away.

As Warren Buffet once said, "Be fearful when others are greedy, be greedy when others are fearful." To me, this means you zig when others zag—a motto I have used in all areas of my life. **Even Google knows this. The world's largest digital marketing platform regularly uses direct mail to reach its high-value prospects.**

Billboard, magazine, newspaper, and TV advertising? All are NOT dead. The fundamental strategic question is whether those channels are where your ideal prospects are hanging out (see Step 6 of the Client Stampede Formula™).

3. If It Works for Them, It Won't Necessarily Work for You (and Possibly Isn't Even Working for Them)

Don't ever make the mistake of copying your competition and assuming they know what they're doing with their marketing. Many companies will see that competitor X is doing a ton of advertising on Instagram, or are promoting their short videos like crazy, so they assume it must be working and that they should be doing it too. Assumptions are very costly to make. **Chances are better than average that your competition might very well be throwing mud at a wall to see what sticks,** or more likely have no idea if a specific marketing campaign is *actually* working or not. They might be chasing shiny marketing objects—new ways of advertising that crop up faster than whack-a-mole at the county fair.

By all means, keep an eye on what your competitors are doing, but never copy them. This just ensures you're blending in with your competitors, not standing out. And certainly don't have a knee-jerk reaction and throw strategy and marketing analysis out the window to "keep up" with them.

4. You Must Advertise MORE THAN Your Brand

Becoming a globally recognized brand with a globally recognized icon like the Apple "apple," the Nike "swoosh" or the green Starbucks mermaid is the gold standard in brand advertising. All you have to do is throw out your logo, and zillions of people know exactly what is being promoted. Honestly, it's like a form of brainwashing. But the idea is simple. If enough people see the same image over and over again and associate it with the same message, voila, you have brand recognition.

But does brand recognition equate to sales, you may be wondering? Ahh, a great question answered in the next step.

When I started my first business, building my "brand image" was the thing I was most excited about. I must have gone through about a hundred different logos, fonts, and colors, looking for just the right combination that would leave my mark on the world. Once decided, then all I had to do was show my brand in enough places, and I would be on my way. Brand recognition would be mine, and running the rest of my business would be easy.

I could not have been more wrong! As it turns out, this misapprehension is what so many companies—large and small—also think. They copy Fortune 500 marketing, thinking that's what's going to get them their big sales breakthrough, when the truth is it took them hundreds of millions or billions of dollars in marketing budget, and sometimes multiple decades, to achieve brand recognition.

As I had neither millions of dollars to hand, nor decades to wait, I figured there had to be a better way. Fortunately there is. It's called 'Direct Response Marketing', and it's worthy of a deeper discussion which we'll have in the next step.

If you can't wait that long, here's a quick summary of Direct Response Marketing:

It means two things: 1) no ad ever goes out simply advertising a brand; it must also contain an irresistible offer. 2) the results of every ad are tracked and measured, so you know, without the shadow of a doubt, which of your ad campaigns are bringing you buyers, and which need to be jettisoned and reformulated.

Brand recognition then is not achieved by simply advertising a brand and hoping that will make the orders come flooding in. **It's accomplished as a happy by-product of direct response advertising that ensures accountability of every marketing dollar you invest.**

5. Marketing and Advertising Are NOT the Same Thing

Saying that marketing and advertising are the same thing is like saying a play in a football game is the whole game. Crazy right? Who would say that one or two tactics comprise the entire football game? **Marketing is the whole game.** That is, the behind-the-scenes strategy, player preparation, training, recruitment, and so on, that went into making the game possible.

Great marketing begins with strategy, and includes every aspect, every touchpoint of a product or service, including target market research, product and service formulation, distribution channels (deciding how and when it should be sold), pricing, sales process, customer experience, and so on.

Advertising is just the play. It refers to the shiny, exciting bits, the icing on the cake that people see, not the iceberg beneath that determines if the ads will be successful in making money. There are plenty of advertising companies who will happily take your money and run ads for your company, throwing mud at the wall to see what sticks. Unfortunately, that describes the vast majority of companies in our industry. Don't just run ads without examining the underlying strategy first, and test, test, and test some more, before throwing serious money at them.

So here's the bottom line on marketing vs. advertising. **Doing advertising without marketing is a high-risk gamble at best, a colossal waste of time and money at worst.**

Doing marketing but no advertising will get you snail's pace growth. To dominate your market, you need both working hand-in-hand. Which brings us to the Client Stampede Formula™. Your marketing breakthrough starts here, with the first step: deciding on the 'Who'.

"The most powerful weapon on earth is the human soul on fire."

FERDINAND FOCH

THE CLIENT STAMPEDE FORMULA

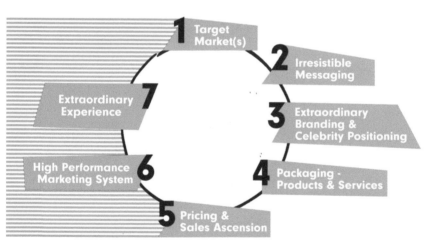

1 Target Market(s)

2 Irresistible Messaging

3 Extraordinary Branding & Celebrity Positioning

4 Packaging - Products & Services

5 Pricing & Sales Ascension

6 High Performance Marketing System

7 Extraordinary Experience

STEP 1

TARGET MARKET

Target Market—
The WHO

"I fear not the man who has practiced 10,000 kicks once, but I fear the man who has practiced one kick 10,000 times."

- BRUCE LEE

This first step—correctly identifying your target market—is the most critical step in the Client Stampede Formula™. If you goof this step, then none of the other six steps will matter. Follow this step carefully, and you'll be on solid footing.

Don't Build A Better Mousetrap

You'll notice this first step begins with the question of WHO. WHO are you targeting? WHO are you serving?

Contrary to what most people believe, it doesn't begin with "WHAT" i.e., what are you selling. This is a crucial distinction because the vast majority of businesses focus on the WHAT first. They spend time "innovating" and coming up with bright new ideas in corporate think tanks.

They get approval and budget to design it, test it, modify it, and then market and launch it, with little thought—if any—to who the product or service is actually going to be sold to, and whether there's a burning market need in the first place. In other words, they create the product first, then hunt around for a market to sell it to.

Can it be done this way? Yes, sometimes—if you have the luck of the Irish. But it's an uphill grind and usually a very slow, expensive, and inefficient way to innovate. This product-first approach is also known as "building a better mousetrap."

Since 1878, the US Patent Office has issued more than **four thousand four hundred mousetrap patents. However, only about twenty of those patents have made any money.** Unbelievably, the US Patent Office continues to receive patent applications for new mousetrap designs every year.

When was the last time you bought a mousetrap? Are you walking around saying, "wow, I wish there was a better mousetrap design because the one I currently have is horrendous"? I know I'm not.

Just because you *think* your company can do something better than a competitor, is not reason enough to do it. You have to find out if that's what your target market actually wants. That's why the Client Stampede Formula™ begins with identifying your target market *first*.

Who Has the Bleeding Neck?

Many years ago, one of my marketing mentors gave me some sage advice. He said, "when identifying a new target market for a client, you could have a thousand possibilities. But look to see who has the *bleeding neck*. Whoever has the most *urgent need*—like the guy who's got a gash in his neck, spurting blood, and running around looking for medical supplies that you happen to sell. That's your best target market."

I never forgot his advice, and as a result, it has helped me to help a lot of companies make a lot of money.

In other words, all target markets are not created equal.

Just because there is an opportunity there, doesn't mean you need to leap on it. Sit back. Do your homework. **Be strategic.** Your best target markets are going to be those who have the most urgent, unmet need.

Ideally, they are the people who are already running around looking for the solution you are offering.

This is very helpful when you get to Step 2: Irresistible Messaging, because you don't have to explain to a target market why they need what you're selling.

They already know they need it and are looking for the best place to buy it.

If you're in a very cutting edge or emerging technology field, this isn't always possible. Your marketing then has to work extra hard because you first have to educate prospective clients about why they need your product or service.

For example, when we're marketing a blockchain technology solution for a client, we can't assume everyone in their target market knows what it is, or why it's light years ahead of other technology storage solutions. As a result, there is a lot of education-based marketing that needs to happen first before a sale can be made. So it will take longer to gain market traction, and likely need a larger marketing budget due to the education component.

Specialist Not Generalist. There Are Riches in Niches

As we discussed earlier, everyone is not your target market. Just because all people have a heartbeat and a wallet does not mean your company should consider them prospective customers.

I know this goes against every left-brained logical thought, which would have us believe the wider the net, the more chance you have of catching the most fish.

Casting your net as wide as possible only works well in fishing, not marketing.

Here's why:

The wider your target audience, the more generic (bland) you have to make your marketing message in order to appeal to everyone.

The more generic your marketing message, the harder it is to attract attention, and the easier it is to get lost in a sea of "sameness." Your marketing will look and sound the same as everyone else's. Blah.

The more blah your marketing message, the harder it is to attract attention, and the fewer sales you'll make.

The fewer sales you make, the more money you'll have to spend on your marketing just to meet bare minimum numbers.

It's a vicious circle.

Can it still be done? Yes, with the right product, service, marketing, and a very, very generous marketing budget. But why even consider this when there's a far faster way that will get you a much bigger ROI on your marketing dollars?

Still not convinced? Let's work through an example.

The Sock Conundrum

Pretend your company sells socks that, in theory, anyone could wear. You decide that because of this, everyone is your target market because everyone needs socks! You wisely choose not to focus on the entire world of sock wearers (a target market just under eight billion), but just within the USA.

The USA has a population of three hundred and thirty million people. That's still a giant and hugely diverse target market. If it cost you $1 to get your ad seen one time, by one person, *then it would cost you $330 million to reach your target market one time.*

That's a big problem because (a) research shows it takes an average of seven touches before a consumer will take action to buy and (b) it costs $330 million to reach a prospect one time.

So, having a target market that big and general is like spitting in the ocean—you're not even going to make a ripple.

Instead, you need to research all the various buyers of socks, and the various uses of socks, and focus on identifying deep, profitable niches. Instead of trying to be all things to everyone (the minnow in the ocean), you're going to focus on dominating niches and become the big fish in a small pond.

So, back to our sock case study, here are some examples of deep profitable niches of sock wearers.

You'll see that in some niches you can drill down even further into micro-niches:

- Running – long-distance, corrective, light
- Equestrian – dressage, Western, show jumping, endurance, trail
- Skiing – Alpine, cross country, downhill racing
- Golf – women's, men's

You get the idea.

Instead of using that $330 Million to market to each person one time, I'd take a small fraction of it and use it to market to each of the people in the deep profitable niches twenty times instead.

Design your marketing strategy to seek out deep, profitable niches, so you can dominate these.

Ten Reasons to Focus On Serving Deep Profitable Niches Instead of Trying to Serve Everyone

1. Your customers want to work with specialists, not generalists
2. The competition reduces the higher up you go
3. It's much more profitable—higher ROI—the more you specialize
4. You'll build your brand and become a major player, faster
5. You can charge higher prices (now you're a specialist, not a generalist)
6. You can more quickly identify underserved burning needs for new product and service development
7. Your referral rate will increase
8. Your speed to market can now be days and weeks, instead of months or years
9. You'll be whistling Dixie all the way to the bank, no longer fighting for crumbs in your marketplace

There's a List for That

There's a joke in marketing circles that goes something along the lines of "if you need to find the names of all the 47-year-old men living in Idle Creek, Indiana, with a golf handicap of ten or less, who own a blue-eyed dog with three legs called Shep, there's a list for that."

It might not be a big list, but it exists. It's sad but true that privacy in the world, and America especially, is dead. As a marketer, I love this, because it means you can drill down and niche micro-target like never before. But as a consumer, *I despise it*, especially when

Big Tech and many, *many* others are collecting our info without our permission and selling it every way possible.

In 2020, Facebook, one of the worst privacy perpetrators, agreed to pay a $550 million settlement over a lawsuit claiming it illegally collected millions of users' biometric data without consent. Mark Zuckerberg has gone on record to say that due to the rise of social media, users no longer expect privacy!

I'll leave this raging debate alone for now. **But know that we live in an age of unprecedented data collection and behavioral tracking.** As marketers, we have tools at our fingertips that the advertising geniuses of a hundred years ago would have never dreamed possible. Which brings us to a very important question.

What Kind of Customers Do You Want?

If you asked a hundred different CEOs, from start-ups to global industry leaders, to raise their hand if they wanted more customers, just about every hand in the room would go up. But be careful what you ask for. Not all customers are created equal.

Some customers are a dream to work with. They happily pay the highest prices in return for excellent value, and are highly appreciative of you and your team. These are the most valuable and obviously the most sought-after customers in your market.

Other customers are at the opposite end of the spectrum. They groan about every little thing. They penny-pinch and are hugely price sensitive. Even though they bring in a fraction of the revenue of your more valuable customers, they are often four times the work and four times the headache.

Let's briefly discuss the different kinds of buyers in each market.

The Customer Pyramid

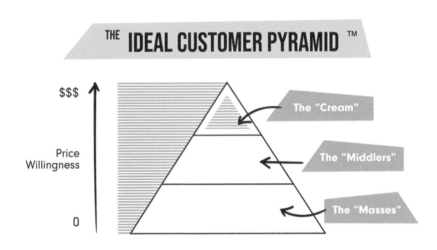

As you can see, there are three levels of customers in the pyramid:

1) The bottom level is what I call "The Masses." This level has the largest number of customers in it, but these people are also the most price-sensitive, the least loyal, and frankly, the most work. For quick reference, I also refer to this level of customer as the Walmart customer. **If your business is serving these people, then God Bless you—you are in a volume game with cut-throat pricing.** It's a race to the bottom. You need to transform your marketing and your brand (using The Client Stampede Formula™) as quickly as possible to start appealing to the middle tier of customers.

2) The middle level of customers and prospects in any market is what I call "The Middlers." They are not your premium customers, but they are not your bottom-of-the-barrel customers either. These buyers are somewhat brand-loyal and are prepared to pay higher prices for products and services they *value*. There are still substantial numbers of these kinds of buyers in each market, but because your

margins are higher, it takes fewer Middlers to make you more money than it does to serve large numbers of the Masses, where it's tough to make a profit.

3) The top level of the pyramid is "The Cream." These buyers are the most discerning, and it takes sophisticated marketing and a longer time to win their trust, but once you've got it, they are loyal, appreciative, and will keep buying again and again. Price is usually the last consideration in their decision-making process. They are fiercely brand-loyal and do not easily substitute one brand for another, but you have to earn their trust every step of the way.

CEO and Entrepreneur Burnout

Whenever I come across a CEO or entrepreneur suffering from burnout, nine times out of ten, it's because their business is aimed at the wrong kinds of customers. They're either serving "the Masses" in their chosen market, or they are targeting a niche they don't enjoy serving. Either way, it's time for a *customer upgrade*.

Knowing who you don't want to work with is just as important as knowing who you do want to work with.

Who Are Your Dream Clients?

If you could wave a magic wand and fill your business with ideal buyers—and dream clients—who would they be? What would they do? What would their interests be? Where would they hang out? What organizations would they belong to? And so on.

My definition of an ideal buyer is someone who is a pleasure to work with, who is highly appreciative of your organization's skills and expertise, who has a burning need for what you offer, *and* who has the money or budget to pay you.

You can, of course, have more than one kind of ideal buyer.

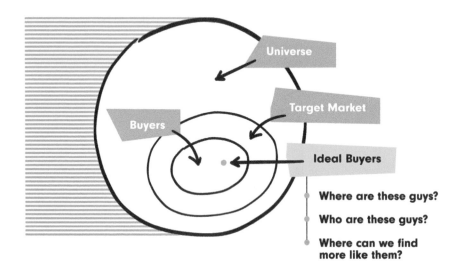

And within the same business, you can have different ideal buyers for different products, different services, and multiple business verticals. However, this is getting into more advanced marketing, so right now, let's just keep things simple by answering two questions:

1) What is your target market?

2) Who are your ideal buyers?

When we first start working with a new client, a minimum of 55% of my team's time is spent doing in-depth market research—about the client's business, their current target market(s), new target market(s), industry trends, competitors, and most importantly, their ideal buyers. This groundwork has to be done very thoroughly *first*, before applying the rest of the Client Stampede Formula™ to their business.

You have to research your ideal buyers so well that you feel like you could invite them to Thanksgiving dinner, and almost predict what they're going to say *before they say it.*

This intimate level of knowledge is essential in the other six steps, especially when building your organization's Marketing Engine in Step 6, and getting your messaging right in Step 2.

Making Your Ideal Buyer Real—Creating Your Avatar

Whether you are selling b2c or b2b, there's a human decision-maker at the receiving end which your marketing message has to connect with, for them to trust you and make a purchase. *Businesses don't buy things. People do.*

Creating an avatar (a fancy way of saying an ideal customer profile) will help laser focus all your marketing and messaging, and provide exponentially better results. For example, instead of saying your target market is professional women, ages 30-45 with interest in losing weight and an annual household income of $100,000 or more, consider changing it to this:

Sarah, a 33-year-old, work-from-home Business Manager, mother of two who has a gym membership she never uses.

Here's what Sarah might look like:

Now that you have a face and a description of your ideal buyer, suddenly your thinking shifts to specifics. You're no longer thinking about marketing "to the masses." Now your approach pivots—this is one busy lady! How can we help her? How can we best connect with her through our marketing? What will she likely pay attention to, and what will she ignore? And so on.

Don't Make Shaquille O'Neal's Multi-Million Dollar Mistake

I read once that the word assume means you're making an ASS out of U and ME. In marketing, it is CRITICAL that you don't make assumptions. The most common assumption is that you, or your marketing team, are your ideal buyers.

Shaquille O'Neal said it best when he discussed his single biggest business mistake. What was his worst decision? Turning down a deal with Starbucks, because he thought, "Black people don't drink coffee."

"I'm always the guy who if I don't believe in it, I can't do it," Shaq said. "That was one of my worst business decisions, because now in every town, on every corner, in every city, you see a Starbucks." That was an expensive assumption, Shaq. The deal ended up going to Magic Johnson, who later sold his interest in 105 Starbucks stores back to the company for an estimated $27 million.

Can You Have More Than One Target Market?

Yes, absolutely. But remember, each target market needs its own strategy, its own special messaging (discussed more in upcoming chapters).

It's best to focus on one target market by asking yourself, "which is the lowest hanging fruit that I can easily reach with the biggest possible upside?"

Start with this market first. Build out your Client Stampede framework, and then repeat the 7 Step process for each new target market.

Need help applying this to your business? Download a copy of my Client Stampede Business Blueprint and Diagnosis Tool. It's free and will help you unpack the basics of how to apply the Client Stampede Formula to your business today. Go to **www.ClientStampedeBook.com**

Case Study: A Top-Ranking Financial Advisory Firm Who Wanted More High-Value Clients

In the personal finance service industry, the holy grail of marketing is having a marketing system that can consistently *attract high net-worth individuals*. This is usually defined as anyone with investable assets of $500,000 or more. Our client was consistently ranked in the top 50 privately held financial services firms, but growth had plateaued. The competition was fierce, and their marketing costs had ballooned with no discernable effect on new client acquisition. In other words, their marketing had stopped working. After poring through their past advertising campaigns and researching their industry and target market, it was obvious what had happened. Their ideal buyers had grown more sophisticated with their expectations, and the firm's branding and current marketing messages were falling flat.

We then divided the firm's target market into three specialist niches we had identified as being the most profitable. Client confidentiality prevents me from sharing the exact details, but in general terms, let's just say it was widows, golfers and equestrians aged 60 and over, with $500,000 or more of investable assets.

We then created three separate websites underpinned by three separate marketing engines that only catered to that specific niche. For example, if you were in the equestrian marketing funnel, you would never know that the firm was also a specialist in helping golf enthusiasts manage their assets, etc. Each engine had the same components (e.g. ten monthly videos, twelve monthly blogs, four articles, a book, four white papers), but each marketing tool was specifically written for that niche. The client was thrilled and we expanded this strategy into eight more niches.

Does your business do over $2 Million in annual revenue? Take my online Client Stampede Marketing Assessment™ and get instant marketing and sales insights to strengthen your business. It's fast and free (it takes less than five minutes to complete), and you'll get instantly emailed your own report.

Visit **www.BolderLouder.com/2Million+**

"Remember the six most expensive words in business are 'we've always done it that way'"

CATHERINE DEVYRE

STEP 2

Irresistible Messaging

Irresistible Messaging. Forget Smoke Signals, Bring in the Freight Train

"I don't know the rules of grammar... If you're trying to persuade people to do something or buy something, it seems to me you should use their language, the language they use every day, the language in which they think..."

DAVID OGILVY

I n 1961, two brothers in Michigan scraped together a $500 deposit and borrowed another $900 to buy a struggling pizza restaurant. Despite being located almost within spitting distance of Eastern Michigan University, the previous owner had not been able to make a success of it. The two brothers worked their tails off and started offering pizza delivery in their beat-up VW Beetle. Within eight months, the second brother was ready to quit and sold his share of the pizza business to his brother Tom in return for the VW Beetle.

Tom kept working like crazy. He knew he had a great location close to campus, but the competition was cut-throat. There were two other pizza joints close by that were aggressively price cutting. He knew he had to come up with what we call in marketing, **A BIG IDEA.**

What Tom did next was genius. After much brainstorming, he came up with a big idea, boiled down to nine words.

Have you ever doubted the power of words to achieve the extraordinary? These nine words became the game-changer for his business. In fact they were so powerful they enabled Tom Monaghan to grow Domino's Pizza into a global billion dollar pizza franchise. One big idea, conveyed simply and irresistibly. Curious as to what words could be so powerful?

Fresh, hot pizza in thirty minutes—or its free.

You'll notice the simplicity of his statement. Tom didn't try to make his business be all things. There's no statement that the pizza is made with the highest quality ingredients or made from a secret family recipe in Italy. Tom didn't even promise his pizzas would taste good (although obviously, they needed to for people to buy more than once).

It was Leonardo Da Vinci who famously once said, "simplicity is the ultimate form of sophistication". This is especially true in marketing. BUT …

The words you choose to represent your business can be the difference between failure and success.

The Power of Great Copywriting

Do you know what copywriting is? No, it has nothing to do with trademarks or intellectual property, but everything to do with *great advertising that sells.*

Copywriting is the art and science of persuasion through written words.

Do you think a two-page sales letter can generate over $2 billion in revenue? It can, and it did for the Wall St Journal. Written in a conversational tone, the sales letter told the story of two young, equally ambitious men who wind up making different choices – one who becomes the CEO of a large company, the other staying in a small managerial job (the winner of course had a subscription to the Wall St Journal for the last twenty-five years, the loser – did not).

The letter starts out like this:

Dear Reader:

On a beautiful late spring afternoon twenty-five years ago, two young men graduated from the same college. They were both very much alike, these two men. Both had been better than average students, both were personable, and both - as young college graduates are - were filled with ambitious dreams for the future.

Recently, these men returned to their college for their 25ᵗʰ reunion …

 You can download a copy of the sales letter as part of the other free marketing tools you'll get when you visit **www.ClientStampedeBook.com**.

You saw how nine words transformed the financial trajectory of Domino's Pizza.

I learned the power of copywriting first hand when I accidentally wrote a winning advertisement for an outdoor furniture company when I was 22. As a result of my ad, the company sold out their entire inventory for the promotion's luxury chaise for the first time ever. I say *accidentally* because I had no clue what copywriting was, let alone how to harness its power in a magazine ad. You can imagine my panic when the company hired me immediately again, expecting me to replicate my first success! That's when I had to get serious about studying copywriting. Even today, I'm still amazed at how just switching up two words in a headline can triple (or neuter) the response rate to an advertisement.

I'll let you in on a little secret. When we're rebranding a client's business, even though the thing they're usually the most impressed with is their new design, 75% of their marketing power doesn't come from this. **It comes from the messaging.**

Mark Twain said it best with his famous quote, "the difference between any word and the right word is like the difference between lightning and lightning bug." So, take your time in this step to get your messaging right – and make it irresistible to your target market.

1. LET'S START AT THE TOP. HOW POWERFUL IS YOUR TAGLINE?

You probably already know what a tagline is. It's the statement that usually appears just below a company's logo, which sums that company up in two seconds or less.

Here are some famous taglines you're probably already familiar with:

Nike – Just Do It

Disneyland – The Happiest Place On Earth

Dollar Shave Club ¬– "Our blades are f***ing great. Shave Time. Shave Money."

Wheaties – The Breakfast of Champions

De Beers – A Diamond is Forever

BMW – The Ultimate Driving Machine

A tagline is the most valuable marketing real estate you have. In the three seconds your target prospect has to glance at your company, what will they remember?

The Irresistible Messaging Acid Test

When someone looks at your logo and reads your tagline, is it immediately evident what business you are in, and what your competitive advantage is? If your business passes the test, congratulations! Frankly, you are a rare breed!

If your business doesn't, then don't worry. It might be time to do a strategic overhaul of your messaging as a foundation for a rebrand. After fifteen years of using the same messaging, that was the case with our agency. I'm going to lift the lid and reveal what we did. In our situation, even our name didn't fit anymore (or pass the acid test), which is a situation you might be facing too.

A Client Stampede Secret: If you're looking at rebranding your business and completely changing the name, ensure that you keep the domain (website address) of your old business and forward it to your new domain. That way, old customers and old prospects can still find you, and your competition can't buy it and claim your old traffic for themselves. Conversely, if you hear of one of your competitors going out of business, make an offer to buy their domain name so you can grab their online traffic!

Remember that a .com domain is perceived as far more valuable (and professional) than a .net, or a .biz (avoid at all costs). Use .co or .io only if you are in the technology industry, otherwise, it just looks weird. Remember also to buy the domains related to your primary domain that are misspelled (again, so people can find you, and your competition can't buy it and grab that traffic).

Pop Quiz: How Powerful Is Your Tagline?

1. Is it obvious from the name of your business and your tagline, what business you're in? Or does it need further explanation?

2. Does it sound completely different to your competitors?

3. Does it capture curiosity?

4. Does it contain a big promise that is appealing to your target market?

5. Is it short and to the point—ideally ten words or less?

Most would stop here in terms of irresistible messaging. Chapter over. But not us. We're just getting warmed up. Why? Because the strength of your messaging establishes value.

The stronger your marketing message, the higher your perceived value, which is especially important for enabling you to charge higher prices and freeing you from having to compete on price ever again.

Next step? It's time to identify your secret sauce.

2. WHAT'S YOUR PROPRIETARY PROCESS?

In 1967, a McDonald's franchise owner, Jim Delligatti, came up with his double patty, triple bun creation. But he needed the perfect sauce to top it off. By 1968, the Big Mac was launched nationally and featured a signature "Special Sauce".

This became known as the Big Mac Sauce recipe "72" and in 1974, the Special Sauce was used in the famous advertising campaign: "Two all-beef patties, Special Sauce, lettuce, cheese, pickles, onions, on a sesame seed bun."

Over the years, there has been much speculation on exactly what goes into the McDonald's Secret Sauce recipe. Even today, if you search online, you'll find a surprising amount of commentary about what it is and isn't, even from media news outlets.

The genius in all this of course, isn't what goes into the secret sauce. It's the fact that McDonald's *has* a Big Mac secret sauce that everyone knows about. This is the thing that prevents any other competitors from replicating the Big Mac.

And so it must be with your business. What is your proprietary process? Believe it or not, just about every company has one. Or *can* have one with a little strategic thought and some tweaks. But it can be hard to identify if your secret sauce is right in front of you.

The bottom line is that in order to create irresistible messaging and prevent your business from being copied, you HAVE to have something that is *totally unique to you.*

Don't be afraid of being transparent with your proprietary process. It's yours. Be proud of it. And as Ray Kroc said about his McDonald's secret sauce and the risk of being copied, "we can innovate faster than they can imitate."

3. CREATING A REVERSE-RISK, BOLD GUARANTEE

Here are the five major reasons why people don't buy:

1. No need

2. No time

3. Too expensive (which means either you have a target market Step 1 problem, or you have a marketing message Step 2 problem)

4. No hurry—they'll buy it in their own time when they're ready

5. They don't trust your company—your sales reps, customer service or marketing promises

The biggest of these is #5, a lack of TRUST. Your target customers simply don't believe what you're saying, and are dead scared of being stuck with a lemon. Frankly, who can blame them? We've all got a long list of disaster stories and battle scars in this area—companies we've bought from who let us down, or even outright lied or cheated their way into making a sale.

I recently had just such an experience when renovating a horse barn on a property we'd recently moved to. The barn had been built in the European tradition and had excellent bones with soaring cathedral-like ceilings, and massive one thousand pound fifty-foot swing doors. But it lacked the basics like matted stalls, box fans, LED lighting, and had a lot of chewed wood. I ended up hiring a contractor who was also the husband of a woman I went horseback riding with on a fairly regular basis. Unfortunately, it turned out to be a complete disaster, and everything that could have gone wrong did. Not only did the contractor and his team do a terrible job, but they took three times longer than planned, costing me twice as much, and when I finally blew my top and fired them with the project only half-finished, he stole my credit card information and charged $6,000 worth of electrical supplies to it at a local store. He's since had criminal charges pressed, and it goes without saying that his wife is no longer my riding buddy. But this is an extreme reminder of what your prospective buyers might be thinking before they commit to buying from you. Whether they're buying a new pair of leather shoes or investing in a $750,000 piece of machinery, they worry they're going to get stuck with a lemon.

Take this fear away by reversing the risk with a guarantee. Many retail stores do this, offering a full refund in 30 days. Most are cheap and don't refund your return shipping, or they might charge you a restocking fee. This is ridiculous.

You might be thinking, "but we're in the business of selling XYZ; we can't guarantee that because we can't control that."

That's ok.

Create a guarantee that controls an unconditional money-back guarantee on one key product or service. Here's an example of ours

98% of all our new client relationships begin with a one-day Business Transformation Consult, with me personally, at my current base consulting rate of $19,860. At the end of our day together, one of three things will happen:

1) We will have had a productive day together, and you'll take away the strategies and techniques we discussed to apply on your own;
2) There will be a project or projects that you'd like our help with, in which case 50% of the day's consult is creditable towards this bigger project or projects, or;
3) You feel that the day together was unproductive, in which case I will cheerfully refund your consult fee.

So, how can you reverse the risk for a customer? Here are some examples of different kinds of guarantees.

1. The Lifetime Guarantee
2. The Free Trial Guarantee
3. The First-Time Guarantee
4. The Happiness Guarantee
5. The Double Your Money Back Guarantee
6. The Fun Guarantee

The next step is to refine your messaging to motivate your prospects to respond to your advertising and create a sense of urgency.

4. MAKING A LIST OF IRRESISTIBLE OFFERS

Unless you create a sense of urgency or scarcity for your prospects, people are only going to take action when they're good and ready. Which is often never, because they simply forget about you, unless you have your marketing spigot turned up high.

If I had waited for a "buyer to be ready" to buy my house in Los Angeles during the last crash, I would still be waiting…

You need to reverse things on this front. The way to best do this is to create irresistible offers.

The Snowstorm-Armchair-Flying-Slipper Test

What makes an offer irresistible? Apply this test.

Your prospect is sitting at home, in his or her slippers. They are outstretched on their favorite recliner, and their butt is practically glued to the seat as they watch the next exciting episode of [insert appropriate show for your target audience]. Their dog/cat/ gerbil is asleep at their feet. Pizza is half-eaten. There's a raging snowstorm outside.

Is your offer so irresistible it makes your prospect yell "yippee" at the top of their lungs, launching mid-air in excitement off their La-Z-Boy, sending slippers, mammal and half-eaten pizza flying? Will they grab their wallet, coat, and keys and brave the blizzard to drive to the store to buy what it is you're selling?

If the answer is yes, you have a winner. If it's no, sharpen your pencil and keep brainstorming. The closer you can get to this, the faster your sales numbers will explode.

5. WHAT IS YOUR STORY?

Gordon Ramsay grew up dirt poor in the housing projects around Scotland with an alcoholic father and a fierce desire to become a pro-football (soccer player). Instead, he became one of the world's most famous chefs with a restaurant and media empire estimated to be worth over $100 million.

Kathy Ireland was paying her way by modeling, gracing the covers of just about every famous magazine in the world. Despite becoming one of the world's most famous faces, she was unhappy with just being the "glorified salesperson." While her fellow models were spending their paychecks on big houses and designer gear, Kathy would show up to shoots in humble sweatpants, meanwhile investing her money in selling a line of socks. That marked the beginning of her billion-dollar licensing and retail empire, outselling even Martha Stewart.

Every business has a story. Every product has a tale. There is another unique aspect of your business that no one else can replicate. Find your story, or stories, and use them liberally in your marketing. Their importance in building trust and a connection with your prospects cannot be overstated.

6. GIVING BACK

Owning a business puts us in a unique position. As entrepreneurs we can make a difference by creating jobs and opportunities, donating to worthy causes, or giving a hand up. If you started your business as a way to give back, that's awesome, but remember - first and foremost, the job of your business is to *make you money. Lots of it. Only then can you do as you wish with your money.* The job of your business isn't to fuel the local economy, or create new jobs or any of those other noble altruistic causes.

It's single goal is to serve you and make you money. It drives me crazy when someone tells me the goal of their business isn't to make money – it's to help others. How can you help others if your business is struggling to make payroll or having a cashflow crisis? *Running a successful business and making lots of money needs to be your primary focus no matter how noble your reasons for doing it. Only then can you have the freedom to help others.*

And, if your company is giving back and helping others, it's a great idea to incorporate this into your marketing message.

Here are two reasons why you might want to do this:

Your customers care that you care

a. A study conducted by Echo Research revealed that more than 90 percent of consumers would switch to a brand that supports a good cause. Additionally, if your target market includes Millennials, the same study revealed more than 85% of millennials correlate their purchasing power to the responsible efforts a company is making. Patagonia is one of my favorite companies—not just for their excellent quality outdoor gear, but for their relentless innovation in "Giving Back." It's one of the most comprehensive giving back programs I've ever seen, which in turn makes me thrilled to spend $450 on an overnight-sized backpack because I know that a percentage of their profits is donated back to environmental initiatives I care about. Their Worn Wear resell site that sells used Patagonia gear reduces landfill, and I know my new backpack also features more sustainable material—a desert shrub-based rubber to replace traditional petroleum-based waterproof materials. As you can no doubt guess, by putting "Giving Back" front and center of their strategic planning and Irresistible Messaging, Patagonia has consistently grown its revenue in leaps and bounds.

Your team REALLY cares that you care

b. Participating in philanthropic initiatives helps employees feel good about themselves and proud about where they work, which in turn builds loyalty. When employees don't feel connected to their job, they make less of an effort and, well ... we all know the impact this has on our businesses.

c. So, what causes are you passionate about in your organization, and what creative ways can you come up with to give back? One of our clients closes their office for a day, and everyone helps out at a local soup kitchen. Another pays their employees to volunteer their time building houses at Habitat for Humanity.

What creative ways can your organization give back and help your team feel they are part of a larger cause?

7. BRINGING IT ALL TOGETHER: CREATE YOUR CORE MESSAGE DOCUMENT

Ok, we've covered a lot in this Step 2. You'll see why getting your messaging down is so important when we start building your marketing engine in Step 6.

Now it's time for you to pull everything together from this step into a document we call the *Core Message Document*. This document will become the messaging bible for you and your team; your guide to writing ad campaigns, website copy, marketing collateral, video scripts, product descriptions, and so on. It is a living, breathing document—the most important marketing document you have, that you can update each year, reflecting any changes to your business and any new irresistible offers you've tested and proven.

Here's the breakdown of what your Core Message Document should include:

1. Business Name
2. Tagline and Unique Value Proposition

3. Proprietary Process
4. Target Market(s) (from Step 1)
5. Bold Guarantee
6. Stories
7. List of Irresistible Offers
8. Giving Back

On we go to Step 3 – Power Branding!

Have you downloaded your copy of The Client Stampede Business Blueprint and Diagnosis Tool yet? It's free and can be downloaded along with some other great marketing tools at **www.ClientStampedeBook.com**.

"I am looking for a lot of men with an infinite capacity to not know what can't be done."

HENRY FORD

STEP 3

Power Branding & Celebrity Positioning

STEP 3
Power Branding & Celebrity Positioning

*"If your business is not a brand,
it's a commodity."*

- ROBERT KIYOSAKI

A man gets up in the morning from his Sealy Posturepedic bed, throwing off his Restoration Hardware linen sheets and knocking his Sony remote. He puts on his Ugg slippers and makes his way to the bathroom for a shower and a shave using his Philips Norelco shaver. He throws on his Kenneth Cole Men's Slim-Fit Suit with his favorite Gucci wool and silk embroidered tie and Tom Ford Midnight-blue shirt, and Prada leather Oxford loafers with Hugo Boss socks. He then heads to the kitchen, making himself a quick cup of Keurig. He remembers to grab his Under Armor workout bag, gives his dog a goodbye pat on the head as he adjusts her Barbour reflective tartan dog collar, and jumps into his Porsche Cayman to drive to work. First order of business? Review and approve his company's marketing budget for an upcoming new product release. He scans the numbers, then grabs his iPhone and calls into his CMO (Chief Marketing Officer). "Hey Jill," he says in his classic New York deep drawl, glancing at his Breitling watch, "why are we spending so much money on branding this thing? It doesn't work."

The words "brand" and "branding" are perhaps some of the most widely used but most consistently misunderstood terms in marketing.

Branding Demystified

What exactly is a brand?

A logo?

A tagline?

An iconic image like the grey apple with a bite taken out of it?

An experience or feeling that you're hoping to convey to a customer?

Yes, to all of these. But a brand is *so* much more.

Your logo, tagline, online ads, your website—these are all components of your brand, but without a specific marketing strategy, they're just marketplace noise.

I view a brand as the personality of your business. It is the very heart and soul that will either attract—or repel—prospects and customers at every single customer touchpoint.

Every business interaction is an opportunity to reinforce branding, from the way the receptionist answers the phone, to the vehicles your sales force drives, to the quality of furniture in your showroom, to the location of your office. This is why it's so important that your company's visual identity, and the way you appear in an online ad for example, is consistent not just across marketing platforms *but within the culture of your organization and the passion of your team.*

I'll give you an example. One of the Real Housewives (for privacy purposes, we can't tell you which one) was referred to us to help her launch her new luxury skincare line. Not surprisingly, she was passionate about beauty, so much so that she owned two medical spas which she had helped build from the ground up. The problem was that the customer base for her medical spas weren't spenders on luxury. They were the exact opposite.

Instead of investing in great marketing and branding that would have enabled her to cherry-pick the best clients in her city, to have higher margins, lower volume, greater profits, and fierce loyalty, our Housewife took the wrong advice and instead filled her medical spas with bottom of the barrel clients—the kind who only bought beauty services based on price—from Groupon (the cheapest of the cheap).

These were certainly not the kind of clients who would happily pay $250 for a jar of our Housewife's caviar eye cream. And they were major headaches to have as clients. The business model had been stretched as far as it could go. Everyone was burned out. Not only that but her website looked like it was built in the 1990s and her branding looked like a kindergartener completed it with an iPad. It was a far cry from her personal brand's glitz and glamor on the Real Housewives show.

The business was in dire need of an extreme branding and business transformation makeover. So, here's what we did:

We first created a visual look and feel for the client that accurately depicted her own personal values and her vision for her companies. She wanted glitz, fun, modern, luxury, and vintage Hollywood glamor all rolled into one. These values had to be the kind that would also be attractive to her new, higher-heeled clientele. We redesigned everything, from the logo and tagline, to the website and eCommerce store, to the marketing collateral and packaging for her new products. We also redesigned the medical spas' interiors to reflect the new sleeker branding and to better maximize sales, without being annoying or pushy, and to optimize the client experience. Out with the old, in with the new. The staff all got new, beautiful designer uniforms. Each product and service got its own extreme makeover—we revamped product descriptions, bundled services (see Step Four), and introduced new recurring revenue streams (membership programs).

Then we created a separate branding identity for her luxury skincare line—a pinnacle brand, meaning it was the highest price, most exclusive brand. We created promotional videos that featured huge mansions and grand staircases with our Housewife making her jaw-dropping entrance. Yes, we were pitching the aspirational rich and famous lifestyle that her followers crave!

The result was she had total brand consistency through every part of her business, and consistency with her own personal brand on the Real Housewives franchise.

If we had simply developed her luxury brand of skincare and tried to "bolt" it onto her existing branding, it would have looked like a Frankenstein bride. It would have also damaged her own personal brand and credibility, and it would have turned off any luxury clients considering trying her new skincare range.

So, whether you like it or not, your company's branding is either working *for* you or *against* you.

Don't Underestimate the Power of Great Branding.

If you're looking to tap into new markets, attract a higher caliber of customers, charge significantly higher prices and/or become the business to beat in your industry, a strategic rebrand is what you need.

Your Brand's Evolution

As with most things, there are varying degrees of "branding."

At the most basic level, branding means a new logo, color palette, maybe a new website, and marketing materials. This is where 96% of all branding projects offered, squarely sit.

At the top level is what I call a Power Brand. It used to take many decades and hundreds of millions, or even billions, of dollars in brand advertising to achieve this exalted status. When you think of big global brands like Apple or Coca Cola, they built their brands the long, slow, hard way, but they reached Power Brand status,

The good news is that thanks to technology, and the fact that privacy is dead in America, companies can quickly access previously untouchable markets at lightning-fast speed. A Power Brand can be built in a few years instead of multiple decades, and for a fraction of a cost.

What Is a Power Brand, and Why Do You Need to Become One?

Becoming a power brand means your business becomes "price proofed". Your clients do not buy on price, and the lower prices of your competition are of no interest because they are convinced there is no substitute.

Let me illustrate this principle with two cartons of eggs.

Both products sit side-by-side in the grocery store.

The eggs are the same color.

The egg cartons contain the same number of eggs.

Yet one carton of eggs costs 500+% more.

How can that be possible?

Because buyers perceive on the right, the yellow, brightly branded carton to be of far superior quality and that the eggs come from happier chickens. This happy egg company understands the power of great marketing, perfectly. The one with the boring egg carton does not. It doesn't matter how cheap the boring eggs are going to be, the other carton's customers are never going to switch.

This is probably a good time to segue into marketing and ethics. It would be grossly unethical of the happy egg company just to make up a bunch of BS about their chickens running around free-range and living long, happy lives on family-owned farms if that was untrue.

Great marketing should NEVER lie. It should simply tell the truth dramatically.

How Do You Build a Power Brand?

The good news is that any business can be elevated to Power Brand status, as long as they have a starving market for the products and services they sell. Like people, brands evolve. Some actually go backwards (devolve?)

There are five stages of brand evolution. Where is your business at?

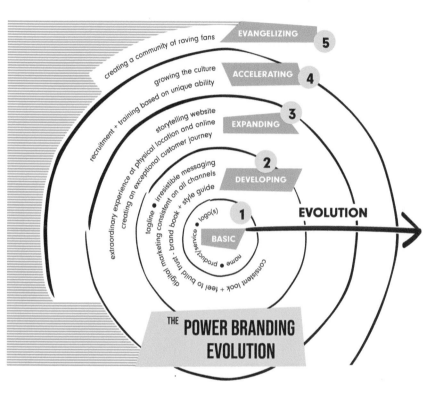

Level 1: The Bare Basic

This is where most businesses sit, including many of the lazier giants who, resting on their laurels, are being upended by gutsy, hungry start-ups who understand the value of building a brand people can identify with.

With a Level 1 brand, you have your overall business name, your individual product and service names, a tagline and a logo. Check. Onto Level 2.

Level 2: Developing

You have everything in Level 1, and it's reflective of your vision, mission and company values. You use consistent Irresistible Messaging (Step 2 of the Client Stampede Formula™) in your marketing communications. And there is a cohesive look and feel across all your marketing—no Frankenstein marketing (schizophrenic marketing). What is Frankenstein marketing? This is where your website has a totally different look and feel to your marketing collateral, which again looks and sounds completely different to your TV advertising, which is different again to Facebook, and different yet again to your billboards. And so on. You get the idea. Frankenstein marketing is usually the result of working with multiple ad agencies, or a combination of in-house/DIY and ad agency. Either way, there is a major disconnect across your marketing which is a barrier to sales. Why? Because consistency BUILDS TRUST—the holy grail of marketing (more on this further down).

Level 3: Expanding

You have everything in Level 2, and you have created a customer journey, both online (through your digital marketing, customer service, and website) and offline (in-store, in-office, in-person interactions). And your physical location(s) are consistent with your brand. For example, think about Pottery Barn. They have a modern, clean and easy to navigate website that successfully imparts a feel of their stylish, yet down-to-earth rustic brand. Whether you experience their brand online, or by browsing through the pages of a catalog or going in-store, everything looks and feels consistent, from the fonts used, to the inviting product descriptions, to the in-store displays. You can take your Pottery Barn experience further by booking an interior design consultation, which provides customers with an even more personalized shopping experience. Obviously, Pottery Barn is a huge brand. You don't have to be huge to build an expanding brand. You just need to focus on creating brand consistency, and an incredible customer journey across every customer touchpoint.

Level 4: Accelerating

This is everything in Level 3 plus culture—that elusive noun that no-one is quite sure how to define. I define it as meaning your entire team—all your employees, your contractors, and your key vendors drink the cool-aid. Miriam-Webster dictionary defines culture as the set of shared attitudes, values, goals, and practices that characterizes an institution or organization.

An example of a brand in the accelerating phase is the new disruptor insurance company, Lemonade. Their track record of delighting customers and employees, and simplifying the process of buying insurance and making claims (think just a few clicks instead of endless phone calls), is taking their industry by storm. Employees are unified in passionately believing complex insurance programs are an unnecessary evil the world should be rid of. The staff call themselves "lemonade makers," and pride themselves on championing simplicity over complexity (the company uses no email; only Slack is used as the method of communication) and in making a real social impact (Lemonade's Giveback program donates all unclaimed premiums to charity).

Level 5: Evangelizing

This is everything in Level 4 plus a real community built with your clients—aka your raving fans. Harry Potter has cultivated a die-hard fandom of Potterheads who know everything from their Hogwarts House to the correct pronunciation of "Wingardium Leviosa."

They're not just customers of JK Rowling's books, they are nuts for anything Hogwarts-related, holding impromptu online meetings to discuss new character theories, or spending $5000+ for a limited edition wizarding robe and magic wand.

Now you understand the evolution of a brand, from ordinary to power. Let's dig into the details of how to take your brand all the way. **Whether you are looking to level up an existing brand, or build a completely new one, the same principles apply.**

The Five Key Components of a Power Brand

1. Eye-popping design

First and foremost, any brand created needs to stand out by looking remarkably better and different to anything else in your market. If you look (and sound) the same as everyone else, you'll blend in, not stand out.

2. Personality-infused messaging (advertising copy)

This is where having a brand story or a brand narrative comes into play.

Compare the messaging for this navy and yellow striped men's shirt.

A typical description would read something like this:

Striped Men's Shirt.

100% cotton. Stitch detailing on the pockets. Tapered fit. Relaxed, casual style for all occasions. Imported.

Using Personality Infused Marketing™ (messaging) it would instead read something like this:

Cabana Shirt

Collins Avenue, Miami. Drinks by the pool at The Savannah. Three-picture deal. Seven points on the back end. These are your terms. The valet brings around a 1955 Lancia Aurelia, tosses you the keys. You're getting the hang of this town. The Cabana Shirt (No. 6646) is the summer shirt of film stars and deal-makers from Miami to Hollywood to the Riviera. Extremely flattering short sleeve, camp collar styling in striped 100% cotton poplin. Imported.

Which shirt would you buy?

The J Peterman Catalog, a luxury clothing catalog that features only product illustrations (no photos), built their entire business on telling product stories and they are exceptional.

If you're not using stories in your marketing, you are missing out on a huge opportunity.

3. Total consistency of look and feel across all marketing

Remember we talked earlier about avoiding Frankenstein Marketing? Why? Because marketing and messaging that looks, feels, and sounds completely different, bolted together, will kill a sale faster than a used car salesman striding towards you on a Saturday morning.

Inconsistency is the death of a sale.

On the other hand, consistency builds trust—the holy grail of marketing. And once you have won a consumer's trust, you will get their repeat business and their referrals forever, unless you either a) stop innovating or b) monumentally screw things up and don't do an excellent job on the recovery.

Here's where having a Brand Book comes into play.

Like the Core Message Document, a Brand Book shows clearly how your brand and your business is to be represented across different forms of media.

From the right and wrong use of your logo and tagline, to the way your brand is to be portrayed in print, digital ads, and even on your website, this is the hymn sheet that everyone needs to sing from, and to never deviate from without authorization. Don't rely on a marketing agency to have your best brand interest at heart. Many are concerned with creating clever ads that look creative or win awards. Your brand is your very, very valuable asset, and it needs to be protected at all costs. Your brand is also a living, breathing representation of your business, and it does need to evolve, not stay locked in a document that was created three years ago and hasn't changed with the times.

What Should a Brand Book Include?

Here's a checklist of some of the most common things to be included:

- Company cliff notes - product and service overview
- Company vision and mission
- Unique selling proposition (taken from your Core Message document in Step 2)
- Brand personality summary
- Logo
- Reverse Logo
- Monochrome Logo

- Logo and tagline
- Logo usage and guidelines
- Icon and watermark usage
- Trademark icon usage
- Typeface
- Typeface usage and guidelines
- Color Palette and Pantone colors
- Hero imagery and guidelines
- Brochure design and guidelines
- Business card design and guidelines
- Website design and guidelines
- etc

You get the idea.

 Branding Case Study: The Global Medical Society with a 1970's Brand Image That Became Industry Leader.

I was flown to Rome to meet with the Executive Committee of a large medical organization; they had a problem. Despite the Society's 50 year history, and the fact it was highly respected in professional circles, membership was down. Its members were aging (75% were fifty and over) and its competitors who previously were only focused in local markets were aggressively pursuing the international market. As you may have guessed, investing in marketing had not been a priority for the organization, ever, and as a result it had an amateur-looking logo that could have been designed in the 70s. Its woefully outdated image was reinforced at every customer interaction, from its clunky, ugly website, to its mish-mash of wildly different-looking marketing materials, and awkwardly worded communications. This was a classic example of an excellent organization not knowing how to articulate what made them so special, and instead being damaged by outdated branding. It was time for an extreme marketing makeover.

We began by doing an global rebrand - starting with designing a logo and a tagline that could be translated successfully into 73 different languages. We created a brand book that unified the Society's color palette and certain use of imagery, and translated this into over a hundred and fifty different marketing tools that could be used by the organization, from newsletters, to tradeshow displays, email campaigns, webinars, new member welcome kits, promotional videos, conference marketing and even a promotional documentary. Their website was rebuilt from the ground up, with two different "sides". The public facing side worked to promote its members and educate the public, the "professional side" was accessible only to members providing them with tools, resources and new ways to connect and mentor each other. Their transformation was stunning, resulting in the largest social media following of all their competitors combined, significantly increased membership and a bi-annual conference with record-breaking attendance.

How to Build a Power Brand on Steroids

In any business, the most valuable thing we have is our relationship with our customers and the trust they put in us.

When you go into McDonald's and order a Big Mac, wherever you are in the world, you have a good idea of what you're going to get. It may not be the tastiest burger in town and it's certainly not made with organic or sustainably sourced ingredients, but it's going to be fast, and inexpensive and taste virtually identical to all the Big Macs you've had previously. That was the goal of founder Ray Kroc from the beginning—he wanted to create a consistent hamburger experience the same way milkshake machines create consistent milkshakes. The messaging is reinforced through all of McDonald's marketing and advertising. They never promise a gourmet burger. They never promise healthy fries.

They promise—and deliver—acceptable tasting, fast, cheap food that's consistent. You and I might say consistently bad, but the 60 million customers a day served by McDonald's franchises would disagree. After seventy years in business, they are experts at winning the trust and repeat business of their customers.

But as we don't have seventy years, seven years, or sometimes seven minutes, what's the best way to grab attention, form relationships and build trust for your brand with a massive number of prospects, in record time?

By using one or both of these strategies in your branding:

1) Use expert positioning tools

2) Create or leverage celebrity

Use Expert Positioning Tools

*"Make your marketing so useful
people would pay you for it."*

JAY BAER

Your brand is your way of reaching and connecting with your customers, and attracting prospective ones.

The deeper your relationship with your prospects and customers, the more valuable and irreplaceable you become to them. This is the "holy grail" of marketing because it effectively makes your competition irrelevant. Instead of having to compete in an overcrowded marketplace where everyone is vying for their attention, you're now the "expert" who has earned their trust. They only have ears for you.

This is done through—drum roll please—*strategic* customer education.

That might sound anti-climactic, but actually, it's mighty powerful.

The best kind of customers for your business are the educated kind. I'm not talking about SAT scores or grad school. I mean customers who are educated about your industry, the products, and services available to them, and they understand how to make an intelligent decision, which leads them to make their own conclusions about who is best to work with—namely your business. This is where the *strategy* comes in.

Here's an example. One of our clients in the real estate industry took their business from $10M to $100M during the four years we worked with them. Over that period, we helped them transition from being heavily reliant on a few key methods of generating business, to a full-scale marketing engine that interwove digital and traditional marketing methods centered around customer education. Not only did this enable us to significantly increase the quality of leads they were receiving, but it also meant we could access brand new markets with pinpoint precision. The leads weren't people who'd been bludgeoned into buying (as so many are when companies become desperate), but they were simply given valuable (strategically written) materials to help them in their purchasing decisions.

You are helping the customer make a smart decision. No one wants to make a wrong decision. No one wants to pay too much. No one wants to end up with a lemon. By educating them on the process of buying, you are doing two things:

1) Building trust

2) Establishing value

There's an old marketing proverb that says "the more you tell the more you sell" (taking the time to answer their objections). This is truer than ever in this fast-paced digital age.

Yes, you can invest a whole lot of money into advertising campaigns which immediately ask your prospects to buy, but why do this when you can load the dice in your favor by asking them NOT to buy. Instead, you offer them something of real value for free, and start building a relationship with them. Your response rate will be much higher!

When we run ad campaigns for clients, on average, our education-based marketing campaigns have a 453% higher response rate than traditional buy-now campaigns, AND they attract a higher caliber of clients.

Expert Positioning Tools, Not Content

BUT, remember that you are not writing to educate per se. You don't want people to read your marketing materials and go "well that was interesting, didn't know that" and then go about their day.

Instead you're writing to persuade, which means you're strategically educating prospects in such a way that provides value and builds desire (to get them to take action).

You've probably heard so many people talk about the need to have content in your marketing—*lots of content.* I personally despise the word content because to me it means something that is very poorly written, it doesn't convey value, and it certainly doesn't create desire. It's just like one of those talking heads that goes blah blah blah, who no one pays any attention to.

The truth is content can actually hurt your business—especially poorly written blog posts and white papers. The companies who create "content" believe that the key to winning customers is volume—pump massive amounts of low quality content into the market to grab attention.

Does this sound like a winning strategy to you?

It must grab attention, glue their eyeballs to the page, and, most importantly, educate them on why choosing your company is the best option. In other words, it explains why your company is the expert.

There are many different kinds of expert positioning tools. The holy grail is of course, a book. Nothing yells "expert" louder than this.

The first best-selling book I contributed to was a game-changer for our agency. It provided immediate personal credibility, business credibility, and a way to help prospective clients sift and sort themselves.

Did our business values and approach to marketing align with our prospects' own beliefs?

Yes? Great! In that case it meant that we might just be a good fit to work together. Now our prospects could take the next step to schedule a complimentary strategic call to see if we could help them.

Or, maybe what I wrote didn't resonate with them? That was great too. It meant they could move on and we didn't waste each other's time scheduling a complimentary call that would not have been a fit.

You see the purpose of great marketing is to act as a giant magnet for your company. It attracts the right prospects to you, and repels the wrong ones.

Yes REPELS.

Arguably this is one of the most essential functions of your marketing. Why? Because you don't want non-qualified prospects wasting your time, or the time of your sales teams. Your marketing needs to sift and sort qualified prospects and repel the rest, so that by the time a prospect reaches out to your team, they have already pre-qualified themselves as being a great quality lead.

A book is a brilliant way of achieving this. A book also has excellent pass-along value; people toss out marketing brochures, but they won't throw out a book. They'll buy copies for their colleagues, friends and family. And so your message spreads

How to Become an Expert by Authoring a Book

Think you don't have the time to write a book? I hear you! Writing a book like this took me eight l-o-n-g months, and it's not even very long!

Honestly, only partially insane people who have a lot to say about a very specialized topic have the time or patience to write a book like this one. For most business owners, it's just not practical and it can feel incredibly daunting, which means it stays in the "too-hard" pile and doesn't get executed.

So what are your options?

1) Press on and make it a priority to write your book. Schedule a regular time to write every day, for example Monday to Friday between 8am-9am. Everyone writes at different speeds but the average production is about 500 "quality" words a day which equates to roughly 1.5 pages. The typical length of a business book can be anywhere between the very short but powerful 10,000 words (for example the worldwide bestseller Who Moved My Cheese), to of course the much longer 50,000 word business book. To give you an idea of what that equates to in size, this book is around 35,000 words.

2) You could hire a ghost writer to write your book for you. A good one who can write eloquently, and capture your voice is going to cost anywhere from $30,000 and up, and the process will typically take about twelve months. You might be surprised to discover how many business owners use ghost writers. Some ghost writers have their names appear on the cover, while others are completely invisible and not mentioned anywhere. If using a ghost author appeals then start taking a closer look at your favorite business books to see which ones might have had "help." There is also an Association of Ghost Authors that you can look up on Google and is a good place to start your research.

3) A third option is "speaking your book" which is the most efficient use of your time. There are many ways this can be done, but it's typically best to use a proven process that will bring the best out of you. One example of this, is the process we use for Lunch Break Books (one of our sister companies.) Here the author is interviewed, podcast style for an hour. The content is then edited, polished and turned into a professionally produced book in a matter of weeks. If you're someone who is much more comfortable speaking rather than putting pen to paper, then "speaking your book" might work best of all.

 Download a copy of Lunch Break Books – How To Become An Expert To Your Dream Clients And Author A Good Book in 60 Minutes by visiting **www.LunchBreakBooks.com** This will give you a good insight into how the "speaking your book" process works and you can test drive it and decide for yourself.

A Word of Warning About Authoring a Book

If you are going to add a book to your company's marketing engine (which I HIGHLY recommend, however you choose to do it) please, please make sure it is a professionally produced, extremely well-written one. Done properly, it will be a game-changer for your business. Done poorly, it could backfire and damage your credibility and your brand.

Other Expert Positioning Tools

A book isn't the only kind of expert positioning tool. Here are some more expert positioning tools to add to your marketing engine:

- Academic articles
- eBooks
- Expertly-positioned blog posts
- Free reports
- Podcasts
- Press releases
- Public speaking and keynote addresses
- Published articles
- Being quoted in the media
- Radio show
- Syndicated columns
- TV documentary

- TV series
- Visibility at high profile charity events

Using any combination of these tools, especially being a published author, will help give your firm expert status (remember Specialist NOT Generalist). And, if you want to up the ante even further, then it's time to harness the power of celebrity.

Adding Kerosene to the Fire—Harnessing the Power of Celebrity

As I'm sure you're well aware, we live in a celebrity-obsessed world. More people look online to see what Kim Kardashian is eating for breakfast than follow the world news. Family doctors lament that their patients look to Dr. Oz for medical advice instead of coming in for a consultation.

Virtually every American consumes something that a celebrity has endorsed, whether it's a shoe, an article, a social media post, a fragrance, a TV program, or a movie. Why do celebrities seem to wield so much influence over us?

Through the research I conducted for this book, and my own experiences working with many celebrities building their brands, the answer is simply 'familiarity'. We trust what we know. We see our favorite celebrities everywhere. We watch their shows, retweet their witty remarks, share their images, admire their training schedules, watch their latest shows, so we think we know them. We have a perceived relationship with them which ultimately (and strangely) is built upon trust. So, how can you leverage the celebrity phenomenon of influence in your organization?

Yes, of course, you can hire a celebrity to endorse your products, use your services, or "be seen" at your premises. Right now, one of the fastest-growing areas of advertising is product placement. For example, that Apple laptop you caught in the background of your favorite film was most likely NOT a production oversight. It resulted from careful strategic planning, complex negotiations, and many hundreds of thousands of dollars changing hands.

The good news is, you don't need to hire a celebrity or pay big-bucks for product placement to get the power of celebrity working for you. Instead, by using the expert positioning tools I mentioned above as much as possible, you can create your own celebrity in your target market.

Ever Heard of PewDiePie?

Probably not, unless you're in your teens, early twenties, are an avid gamer or work in marketing. His real name is Felix Kjellberg, and he's a Swedish social media influencer. With a subscriber base of close to 150 million, he is the most followed YouTuber of all time. He also entertains enormous audiences on Instagram, Facebook, and Twitter, reaching a total following of nearly 200 million across the four platforms. Back in 2010, Felix was just a regular kid who started posting, blogging, and video recording like crazy, carving out a niche for himself.

The point is, you don't have to create celebrity at the Brad Pitt level. As the founder of your company, you just need to be known, extremely well-known, to your target audience.

So now we've covered the nuts and bolts of how to create a Power Brand, and why it's essential to have one.

 If you haven't downloaded a copy of the Client Stampede Marketing Blueprint™ yet, now would be a good time. And yup, it's free! Visit **www.ClientStampedeBook.com**

I'll leave you with one more story that further illustrates the power of branding before we move on.

Stephen King Unmasked: Fame vs Talent

To date, Stephen King's books of horror, supernatural fiction, suspense, crime, science-fiction, and fantasy have sold more than 350 million copies. If you haven't heard of him, you would be one of the few on the planet. Horror novels are definitely not my cup of tea, but his non-fiction book called "On Writing" is one of my favorites.

To tell this story, let's rewind the clock. It's 1977. Stephen King has managed to transform himself from a near-destitute English teacher to a cultural phenomenon. His first three books—Carrie, Salem's Lot, and The Shining—are bestsellers, and his fourth book, The Stand, is nearing completion. Feature film and paperback rights for his work are added to his newfound wealth... Steve is on fire.

But he had a professional problem. He wanted to publish more than the industry standard of one book a year. His editors balked at the idea. Multiple releases would flood the market, they insisted. It would damage the Stephen King brand and cannibalize (i.e. depress) sales.

It was lucky that Steve was an inventive guy who didn't take no for an answer. So he created a pseudonym for himself with a backstory—Richard Bachman, born in New York, ex-Coast Guard and Merchant Marine who finally settled down in rural central New Hampshire, where he ran a medium-sized dairy farm, and wrote at night.

Another reason for using the Bachman pseudonym is that Steve was also curious if his fame (his own personal brand) was the real reason his books were selling so well, or if the reason was in fact, the writing itself. So he published Rage in 1977, followed by The Long Walk in 1979, Roadwork in 1981, and The Running Man in 1982.

Steve did as little marketing as possible.

The result? Sales were meager, and the reader reaction was tepid. No one knew Bachman. He was an unknown writer of apparently mediocre talent. King recalled getting around 250 fan letters a month for himself, and perhaps one a month for Bachman.

The Bachman book Thinner (1984) sold 28,000 copies during its initial run—and then one hundred times as many when it was revealed that Bachman was, in fact, Stephen King. To date, Thinner has sold over 3 million copies.

Moral of the story: The most powerful brand wins—every time.

"Normality is a paved road: it's comfortable to walk but no flowers grow."

VINCENT VAN GOGH

STEP 4

Packaging It Up

Packaging It Up

"Stop selling. Start helping."

- ZIG ZIGLAR

W e've already discussed how your messaging, branding and expert positioning all help to give you a competitive edge in your market. Step 4 of the Client Stampede Formula™ is one of the most overlooked areas of business to innovate in. Possibly because it doesn't sound very exciting.

Packaging. *Yay.*

You will be saying YAY when you see how this simple step works, and how profound its results can be.

There are two aspects to packaging. One involves strategic thinking, the other is all about aesthetic appearance. As always, let's start with strategy.

Why Package up Your Products and Services?

By now, you know your target market. You're intimately acquainted with your ideal prospect—so much so, you could date them with the level of knowledge you've acquired. You know their habits, their strengths, their weaknesses, their fears, their problems, their desires, their hopes, their dreams. You know what keeps them awake at night. And you definitely know how they like to spend their free time. So far, so good.

You also know that the worst position your business can be in is the commodity business, or being perceived as a commodity. By that, I mean you have no brand recognition and your target market believe that what you sell is precisely the same as what the competition sells, so in the absence of any further information, they shop around on price.

For example, let's say you're a plastic surgeon entrepreneur and you own a chain of medical spas. You're ready to invest $500,000 on three facial rejuvenation lasers. You choose the latest and most fantastic laser, sold by a very well-known brand name that people in your target market are actively searching for. Unfortunately, all your main competitors have had the same thought. They also want the latest and greatest facial rejuvenation laser. They've also invested in the exact same laser technology. Now everyone needs to recoup their investment costs fast, before the next new model comes out. This is not good. Unless you come up with a major point of distinction for your laser services, there's going to be a price war bloodbath. So what do you do?

You prevent your target market from making an apples-to-apples comparison by changing the game. You make comparison impossible.

How do you do this? By bundling up products and services together that your target market needs and wants. Time to get creative. This now enables only an apples to artichokes comparison.

 Client Stampede Secret: Bundling services along with products is a great way to add value to your customer, price proof it (the next Client Stampede step) and increase your average transaction size, all in one shot.

Now we've talked about the need to strategically package your products and services together, we need to talk about actual packaging.

The Importance of Packaging the Right Way

Invest in great packaging for your products and services. Whether you're selling actual goods that require physical packaging, or in-person services, or digital sales, your packaging and the strength of your graphic design is yet another way to differentiate yourself from the pack and increase perceived value. Even more than this, your choice of packaging is proven to result in different psychological experiences.

Take a look at these two products.

Both are gum, but they are packaged completely differently. One looks stock-standard. Like every other gum package on the shelf. The other? Innovative, fun, cool.

Your customer's perception is critical; their perception is their reality.

Beer—from a bottle or a can?

Philadelphia cream cheese—silver foil bar or plastic tub?

Too often, I see organizations set aside skinny budgets for packaging development, not realizing their extreme importance. When we design packaging for clients, we usually do thousands of micro-online tests to help us choose designs with the best conversion rates. For example, does red convert better than blue? Does one style of font appeal more than another? Which image attracted the greatest number of clicks?

If you think you only sell services with no physical packaging to offer, think again. All your marketing collateral is "your packaging", as are the presentations your salespeople are making. Do they use an iPad on the road and process orders electronically? Do they use beautiful-looking presentations and videos? Or are they still tied to messy paper order forms and a dog-eared-looking spiral-bound folder? Are your brochures and marketing materials, including your business cards, excellent quality with sleek graphics and clear calls to action?

If yes, great—that's also your packaging.

If no, don't worry, take a read of Step 5 and dive right in.

Keep It Simple

Last time I was in the grocery aisle, I counted over 100 different kinds of canned soup. Canned soup! Not sure when shopping for soup became so difficult, or so overwhelming. It could take one person fifteen minutes of standing there alone just trying to read all the different options. Chances are pretty high they would get frustrated and leave the store soupless, opting instead for a deli sandwich on the way out.

The trick is to package up your products and services to make things easy for your prospective customer, not complicated. The goal always is to make it easy for your customer to say YES.

Many organizations think this means you have to add something continually. Things keep getting added and added. And the options become more and more complex and overwhelming to your prospect. It was Leonardo da Vinci who once remarked "simplicity is the ultimate form of sophistication". So very true. Complexity is the death of a sale.

Keep your packages simple and of high value, ideally always making it easier to say yes than no. And keep your customers wanting more.

Which brings us to Step 5: Price, Price Baby and Sales Ascension.

"If I had asked people what they wanted, they would have said, 'faster horses'."

HENRY FORD.

STEP 5

Pricing

Price, Price Baby and Sales Ascension

"The bitterness of poor quality remains long after the sweetness of low price is forgotten."

- BENJAMIN FRANKLIN

Not long ago, our agency worked with a successful landscaping supply company based in Southern California. It had been a family-run business for three generations. Sadly, the father had passed, leaving his wife and adult son to run it. Fortunately, both were savvy, entrepreneurial and worked well together as the executive team. Over the previous decade, the family had expanded their business into 15 different locations across three states. Year after year, their business enjoyed double-digit growth, sometimes triple-digit. But then, overnight, growth stalled and revenue numbers started to decline. A bigger competitor was strategically buying up all the small landscaping supply companies and undercutting their retail and wholesale prices to barely above cost. It had become a race to the bottom. Who could sell mulch the cheapest?

As you now know, price cutting is the death of a brand and means your business is servicing the bottom of the pyramid—"the masses"—those folks who ONLY buy on price. A race to the bottom price-wise is a race you never want to be in.

It's a race every business with weak marketing is in by default. They don't know how else to get customers, so they cut their prices and make this their irresistible messaging (Step 2 of the Client Stampede Formula™). Their only competitive advantage = lowest pricing.

The problem with this positioning is that there will always be someone hungrier and more desperate than you. Overnight they can slash their prices below yours, and then where does that leave you? Either with no competitive advantage, or with a pricing model that's going to bleed you dry.

Unfortunately, these price-driven customers also happen to be the cheapest and the most stressful/biggest headache to serve. Nothing will burn you out quicker than dealing with this lot. So what should you do instead? Overhaul your marketing and sharpen up your Irresistible Messaging, like we did with this client.

First, understand this simple premise of pricing as stated by Warren Buffet:

"Pricing is what you pay. Value is what you get."

Value-Based Pricing

In other words, customers will only buy your product if they believe that the value they're getting is greater than the price they're paying. Otherwise, why would they buy?

So, getting back to our landscaping supply conundrum, how can you convey VALUE so that people will happily pay more when, in effect, you're selling a commodity?

The answer is to strengthen your marketing message and clearly articulate why you're better and different (Step 2 of the Client Stampede Formula™) and reposition your brand (Steps 3 and 4).

Here's how we did that.

Our team dug into the market research for the retail and wholesale landscaping supply industry. We had worked with a previous client in this field, based in Ohio, so we had a good foundational understanding, but the challenges faced by this company operating multi-locations in So Cal were very different from our client in Cleveland—different market, different price points, different demand, different client expectations, and different growth pain points. Once we'd done our localized research, we started drilling into their various prices and service offerings.

One similarity this business had with our Cleveland client was that their top-selling product, which also happened to have the biggest margin, was mulch. Did you know that not all much is created equal? Some mulch is made from recycled pallet wood that can contain nails, chemicals, even cancer-inducing creosote.

At the other end of the spectrum, other mulch is made 100% from trees—all-natural and shredded to perfection. Speaking of shredding, did you know that the shape of the mulch, and whether it's been shredded, chipped, or bladed, will determine how long it lasts before needing to be replaced?

And what about the dyes used? Some are anything but natural (like that horrible electric red color you see everywhere), whereas other kinds of mulch are dyed using 100% natural vegetable dyes. Some mulch is organic, and others can make a dog horribly sick if ingested.

We then repositioned our client's marketing to be education-based so that their customers could now make a more informed decision. By doing this, we were separating our client's products from the rest of the pack with their marketing message. Value-based pricing in other words. It was a good start, but that was not enough to substantially raise prices in and of itself.

Next, we rebranded their mulch products so that a direct comparison would be impossible. We worked with their sales teams to refine their sales pitches and clearly articulate the differences, which pivoted the "sales process" from a pitch to an actual consult. And finally, to top it off, we worked on Step 7—creating an extraordinary experience for their clients.

We simplified their delivery charges, introduced a guarantee, and created a simple "gift" that was left attached to the door of every retail mulch customer, and we overhauled their wholesale buying program.

We increased prices by 53%-447%, communicated through a carefully crafted communications campaign that used email, social media, radio, direct mail, signage, and video.

The results took even us by surprise. The price hike knocked off the bottom rung of customers—the ones who only price shop—but it increased margin by 50-200+%, meaning our client could afford to lose more than half their existing client base and still make more money.

Over 75% of their clients stayed with them following the price increases, and astonishingly, new business grew by an additional 24% retail and 11% wholesale/commercial. I'll leave you to do the math, but suffice it to say that this business transformation was a home run, and best of all, they had now price-proofed their key products. Which brings us to a very important four-letter word when it comes to pricing strategy.

We All Love FREE But... What's Next?

No matter what anyone says, the word FREE is still the most powerful in the English language. We all know there's no such thing as a free lunch but... when I tell you to go visit our website at

www.BolderLouder.com to discover your Client Stampede Opportunity Score, and receive your own custom marketing assessment and results, you know it's not really free, because you're giving me your email, and your permission to talk you through our marketing. From there, you might decide to buy one of our training courses, or join a coaching program, or request a consult or become a private client.

We're giving away something of real value for free. But it's free with a goal: to build a relationship with you and win your trust so that anytime you have a marketing need, you'll think of us and the Client Stampede Formula™.

What things are you giving away for free in your business, and what's next in your customer ascension? Let's look at the Ideal Customer Pyramid again, but this time let's focus on the vertical axis with price. If you plotted all the different price points of your products and services, what pattern would emerge? Would you be clumped around one price point, or would you be somewhat evenly spread?

Are you giving away things of value for free (or low cost) to build a relationship, establish trust and grow your list? Do you offer pinnacle products and services—the best-of-the-best, total luxury, all-inclusive (whatever your description might be)?

 Client Stampede Secret: No matter what industry you're in, if you don't have a pinnacle product or service, you are leaving a lot of money on the table.

Through my research for this book, and from my own personal experience, it's statistically probable that between 1.4% and 6.2% of your client population will purchase your pinnacle product or service if you offer it to them. They want the best.

There's one key point to remember before we move on to charting your sales ascension:

The further you move away from free and commodity pricing, and the more expensive your prices, the stronger both your marketing message and branding (Steps 2 and 3 of the Client Stampede Formula™) need to be.

This step is about ensuring you are being strategic about your various price points and making it easy for someone to "try" your business by putting a toe in the water without having to dive in all the way.

Would You Like Fries with That? Charting Your Sales Ascension Ladder.

When you generate leads for your business, the hardest thing to win is a client's first dollar. Once you've got a client over that hurdle, it becomes infinitely easier for them to buy from you again and again—assuming you give them a great first experience, of course.

In fact, research shows that's it's seven times harder to convert a prospect into a paying client than it is to get an existing client to buy from you again. Just let that number sink in again—seven times harder!

So, you want to make it as easy as possible to turn your prospects into paying customers as soon as possible, which means selling something at a low price point with low risk. Once you've delivered them an exceptional experience, they'll be back for more, and that's where you need to chart their sales ascension.

But what about the fries? When creating your sales ascension ladder, don't forget to also create your upsell. Go back to the packages you created in the previous step. Can you upgrade these customers to a higher package at only a little extra cost? Can you add on a service or a complimentary product? How would you do this?

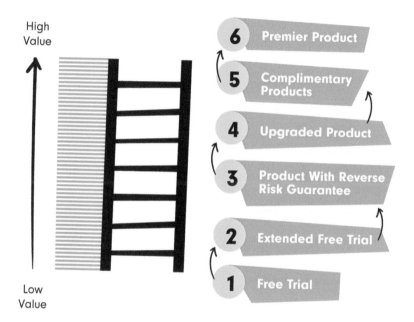

THE SALES ASCENSION LADDER

High Value

6 Premier Product

5 Complimentary Products

4 Upgraded Product

3 Product With Reverse Risk Guarantee

2 Extended Free Trial

1 Free Trial

Low Value

- **Who will climb the ladder?**
- **How will you get them to ascend to the next rung?**

Need help creating your pricing strategy? Go download a copy of my Client Stampede Blueprint Training™ for more easy-to-implement pricing tips. All FREE (yes free, because in return for your email address, I'd like to keep delivering you massive value, so you'll realize the Client Stampede Formula™ has been the missing piece to your success and you'll join our awesome community.) Visit **www.ClientStampedeBook.com** to access your download.

Still with me? You're doing great!

Now let's build your organization's marketing engine. Are we building a Maserati or a Mini?

 ### The $1,851 Per Minute Business Consult

I once had a call with a client who was tearing his hair out over an issue with his sales team. The issue was costing his company millions of dollars in lost revenue and lost customers. We spoke for 27 minutes. I solved his problem and he hung up happy with the information he received. The next day he Fedexed me a check for $50,000, not because my consulting rate is $1851 per minute (I don't have one), but because he was grateful and knows the value of great information in helping grow his business. He didn't associate time with value. That's how Big Players think.

"A tiger doesn't lose sleep over the opinion of sheep."

SHAHIR ZAG

STEP 6

Your High Performance Marketing Engine

Your High Performance Marketing Engine

"I honestly believe that advertising is the most
fun you can have with your clothes on".

- JERRY DELLA FEMINA

The most valuable business lesson I ever learned wasn't from two university degrees (including one in marketing). It wasn't learned from any of the marketing courses I've invested hundreds of thousands in to attend since.

My most valuable business lesson was learned while flipping hamburgers at McDonald's, aged sixteen. That same business wisdom is what's used to build billion dollar companies all over the world, as well as transform small, scrappy start-ups into major players in record time.

Can you guess what the business wisdom is? It can be summarized in four words:

The. Power. Of. Systems.

Within the first five minutes of working at McDonald's, I learned they had a very specific system for inducting new employees. This comprised of introducing us to the hundreds of different systems

McDonald's uses. From the system used to make their hamburgers, ensuring the lettuce and tomato got put on in a certain order (only three rings of onion, not four), to the way you wash your hands (three pumps of soap, lather for two minutes, then rinse), to the number of marshmallows you put on a hot chocolate (fourteen). There is no guesswork. Employees just have to follow the system.

The burgers at McDonald's are never flipped. They are grilled on a special electric griddle that cooks the patty from the top and the bottom, decreasing the cooking time: It takes 40 seconds to cook the frozen patty. Salt and pepper are added to the burger after cooking. While the patties are cooking, the buns are being toasted on a separate electric griddle. The cook uses a spatula to put the patty on the heel (bottom of the bun, not the top). The condiments and pickles are then added to the top of the patty, and the crown (top of the bun) is then added. The burger is wrapped and slid into a heated serving unit, which the cashier puts in a bag and gives to the customer. The total time it takes to prepare a McDonald's hamburger, from taking it out of the freezer to putting it into the customer's hands, is 90 seconds.

Every single thing McDonald's does, has its own system. The way you make the fries, the way you restock the cups. There was even a set system for employees to wash the dishes in the back.

Why is McDonald's so system-crazy?

1) Because systems produce consistent results, meaning that if I go to Auckland, New Zealand and order a Big Mac, it's going to pretty much look and taste the same as the one I ordered in Los Angeles.

2) Systems are massively efficient for maximizing productivity, reducing costs and maximizing profits. It's by having these systems in place that McDonald's has been able to grow to 37,000 franchise locations producing $19 Billion revenue/year.

Behind every uber-successful business lies a dedication to systems: systems for training staff, systems for producing products, sales order systems etc. And, arguably their most important system—a system for marketing—meaning a systemized, reliable method of attracting, converting and retaining new clients.

My experience is that most businesses, large and small, experience wild swings of cashflow in response to high and low seasons. It's either feast or famine, with not much consistency in between.

A marketing system fixes all that.

Here are the other benefits of having a marketing system:

1) It provides you with **a steady stream of highly qualified prospects** who have already sifted and sorted themselves. The ultimate goal of a marketing system is to only attract prospects that are a really good fit, and REPEL the rest. Yes, repel. This means you and your sales team don't have to waste your time talking to tire kickers, people who can't afford your services and/or those buyers who only buy on price and don't value anything else.

2) It **streamlines your client attraction, conversion and retention processes, so no lead is ever wasted, and every part of the client journey is systemized.** Your unconverted leads don't fall by the wayside. Your existing customers don't get treated like second-class citizens because they also get their own set of special offers and initiatives to keep them happy, loyal and engaged.

3) Your conversion rates increase. 90% of the time, when a prospect reaches your conversion process, they have already made up their mind. They just need to confirm their decision, or gain a little helpful incentive to take the next step.

4) Your marketing system can run for you twenty-four hours a day, seven days a week, three hundred and sixty five days of the year. You can dial it up when you need more leads, and down when you need less. Having a marketing system in place puts you in control of the size of your business. Bad economy, good economy, competitive marketplace, small-town—none of this matters.

5) It irons out cash flow and enables you to stimulate demand in slow periods and reduce the flow in busy periods, all depending on your capacity. In other words, a marketing system puts your organization in control of sales, instead of being at the whim of your customer.

It also makes recruiting new staff incredibly simple. Like when I worked at McDonald's, I just needed to learn the system. And if one of your key staff members leaves (e.g. your top-performing sales star), your business keeps on trucking because you have the marketing system. You've got the database of leads, and converted leads, and unconverted leads and the methodologies to convert them. So you find another sales star, plug them into the system and away they go.

Having a marketing system in place means you get to create your own demand – no matter whether it's high or low season, a global recession or a lockdown pandemic. None of these external factors are relevant anymore.

Remember my story about how I sold my house during the recession, to a couple who weren't even looking to buy? I created a marketing system that would attract large numbers of potential buyers, prequalify the serious buyers, and put in place a method of selling to the highest bidder. It was fully transparent, easy to understand, and would enable the top buyers to rise to the top.

I call having a marketing system your marketing engine because marketing is the machine that drives the growth of your business. In my humble opinion, it's the most valuable investment you can make in any business.

So What Exactly Qualifies as Marketing?

My views might be a bit extreme because of the way my brain is programmed, but I see every activity a business engages in, as marketing. This includes the speed with which your team answers your phone, the quality of the chairs your customers sit in, the interior design of your office, the make of vans driven by your workers, the sign in front of your office, the on-hold message on your phone system—everything. Including, of course, all the advertising and actual marketing that your business does. **To me, all of these activities are either growing, or shrinking, your brand, so they're marketing.**

Sometimes this wiring inside my brain can create a pretty awkward situation.

For example, some good friends once invited me to attend church for a band performance their son was playing in.

This particular church had experienced explosive growth and had opened three new locations in the past two years. I was bursting with curiosity to see what their Marketing Engine looked like, and of course also wanted to support my friends. So along I went.

I had hardly set foot in the front door when I was engulfed by three "greeters" whose arms were outstretched, welcoming me as a newcomer to their church. I was given a "welcome kit" and a shiny new

bible and was asked if I could register myself on their "guest list" (i.e., get my contact info so they could market to me), which I politely declined. Not to be deterred, they then handed me a questionnaire asking me to check all the church activities I was most interested in—everything from divorce support groups, to missionary work, to helping run the hot dog stand at their annual family carnival. After telling them that I would hold onto my questionnaire thanks, I was given a knowing nod and smile and told to "enjoy the service."

I made my way into a semi-dark amphitheater with stadium-style seats—the kind that you have to flip down to sit on. Up front was a giant Imax-size screen playing a short film that appeared to prominently feature the two pastors in some kind of modern-day biblical reenactment (they used terms like "Yo" and "Bro"). In front of this was a stage set up with an 8-piece band (including our friend's son), state-of-the-art musical instruments, music production equipment, and recording equipment.

I looked around the semi-dark auditorium. It was crammed full with university students, young families, hipsters, and trendily-dressed grannies. I could probably write an entire book on the marketing lessons from attending this service, but I'll fast-forward and give you the cliff notes version, and the takeaway.

Cliff notes: our friend's son did a fantastic job playing the drums. The walls of the church/amphitheater vibrated, and I'm guessing even the people in the neighboring town had the benefit of hearing the worship music. There was no actual "live" service; we watched the Hollywood-style pastors deliver their message via pre-recorded video. At various times during the service there was the opportunity for people to donate using Apple Pay on their phones. Everyone also got to vote (using their phones) on whether or not they were interested in upcoming programs, and could pre-register instantly for a deep discount (a very smart business strategy on multiple levels). Before concluding, everyone was asked to spread the good word about the church. The social media hashtags came up on the screen along with a selfie of someone holding their branded bible, encouraging everyone to post or tweet their attendance at today's service.

Oh, and free stickers and yard signs were available for people to take home in large supplies.

After the service, I collected my child from Sunday school and I asked her what she learned. She told me that it was the best Sunday school ever! She got a slushie, sang songs, played in the ball-pit, climbed on the climbing wall and got to watch a movie in the kid movie theater. Fun times!

Such a smart business strategy to have the kids BEGGING their parents to go to Sunday school!

In the following three months, I was bombarded with this church's marketing—everything from eMagazines, to new song releases, to live updates from missionary projects. I had three people try and call me, but fortunately I had given them our office number so they couldn't get past my assistant.

Their Marketing Engine was definitely more of a Maserati. It was extensive, extremely well-strategized and powered by a great deal of Marketing Gas (explained further below) – which of course was the reason behind the church's explosive growth!

Its marketing was brilliant. They understood the needs of their target market perfectly and tailored their business model accordingly.

When I chatted to my friends about how incredible the church's marketing was, they looked at me in bewilderment. They never saw any of the church's activities through this marketing lens.

They only saw a well-run organization that was built around service to the Lord!

So now that we've established what marketing is (everything your business does—every touchpoint, every product, every experience) and we've established how critical it is for you to have a Marketing Engine that puts your marketing on autopilot, and puts you in control, what does a marketing system actually look like?

It's broken down into three simple "units":

1) **Attraction:** everything your business does to get a highly qualified prospect to raise their hand as being interested in something you sell. These include all your lead generation strategies, such as digital marketing campaigns, billboard advertising, podcasts, print advertisements, etc.

2) **Conversion:** the process of converting prospects into actual paying customers—your sales process, whether this is a phone call, an in-person meeting or series of meetings, or an online buying experience for example.

3) **Retention:** every marketing activity aimed at keeping your customers loyal, happy, engaged, and buying more, such as an eMagazine, print magazine, direct mail campaigns etc. This is the MOST ignored, yet most profitable area of your marketing engine.

HOW A MARKETING SYSTEM WORKS

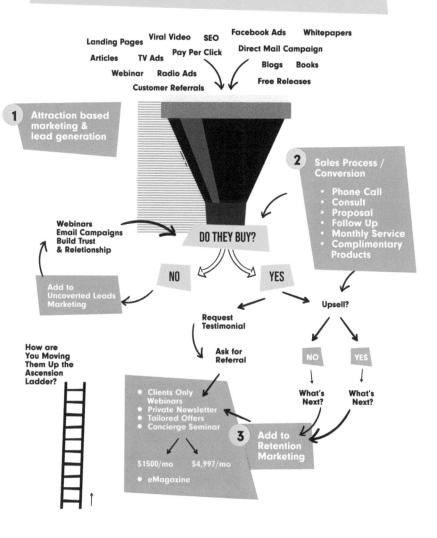

Landing Pages · Viral Video · SEO · Facebook Ads · Whitepapers
Articles · Pay Per Click · Direct Mail Campaign
TV Ads · Blogs · Books
Webinar · Radio Ads · Free Releases
Customer Referrals

1 Attraction based marketing & lead generation

2 Sales Process / Conversion
- Phone Call
- Consult
- Proposal
- Follow Up
- Monthly Service
- Complimentary Products

Webinars
Email Campaigns
Build Trust
& Reletionship

DO THEY BUY?

NO   YES

Add to Uncoverted Leads Marketing

Upsell?

Request Testimonial

NO   YES

How are You Moving Them Up the Ascension Ladder?

Ask for Referral

What's Next?   What's Next?

- Clients Only Webinars
- Private Newsletter
- Tailored Offers
- Concierge Seminar

3 Add to Retention Marketing

$1500/mo $4,997/mo

- eMagazine

Marketing Engine Case Study: The $100 Million Real Estate Portfolio for Sale That Got 16 Offers in Three Weeks.

One of our clients owned a commercial real estate portfolio of student housing accommodation with an estimated value of $100 Million. A serial entrepreneur, our client had spent many years building this portfolio on the side, in addition to several other highly successful businesses that he'd built and sold over the years. After divorcing wife number five, and the economy strong, he had decided now was the time to sell. Except that he despised Commercial Brokers and didn't want to pay one to (in his words) "sit on their ass and do nothing except cash their commission check." I had to agree. The gross incompetence of 99.9% of real estate agents—residential or commercial—is one of my personal pet peeves.

One night we were having a dinner business meeting when he leaned back on his chair, and waggling his cigar at me said, "you know that thing you did in Los Angeles to sell your house? That's what I want you to do to sell my portfolio."

Challenge accepted! It's important to note that no one in our agency was a licensed agent, and the sale of the portfolio was a FSBO—for sale by owner. We were not masquerading as commercial agents. Just like with the house in Los Angeles, we knew we'd need to create our own process, market his portfolio like crazy and put everything on a tight deadline to channel demand and create scarcity. We started with the properties themselves and made each of them as appealing as possible, getting his maintenance crew working overtime to ensure interiors and exteriors were freshly painted, new carpet replacing worn, windows cleaned, new mailboxes and yards that looked color-filled and inviting.

We professionally staged a few units in each property, and hired professional videographers to do many different kinds of video (3D walk throughs, drone footage, etc). We also created videos of testimonials from happy tenants, made videos of the surrounding area for out-of-town buyers, and had professional photos taken. Then we created a prospectus like none other you've seen before. Over 100 pages profiling each property in detail, including rent rolls and neighborhood information. Our Client's CFO even prepared detailed statements of accounts for each property. We wanted to overwhelm a prospective buyer with information, not necessarily for them to look at, but to ensure as much as possible was there for them to look at. Then, we launched the marketing and watched our inbox blow up with queries, questions, and requests for more information.

Queries came from as close as the next town along and as far away as Shanghai. After one of the most intensive marketing campaigns our agency has ever launched, we fielded over 500 inquiries and at the expiration of the deadline, our client had received 16 offers—all with proof of funding. As you can imagine, he was a very happy camper, but ironically he refused them all (eye roll).

Why? All our great marketing had made him fall in love with his portfolio of properties again and he decided he did want to keep them after all, especially now we had helped him determine they were even more valuable (and desirable) than he'd previously thought.

THE TWO CLIENT STAMPEDE MARKETING SYSTEM FUNDAMENTALS

FUNDAMENTAL ONE: Build the Quality and Quantity of Your House Mailing List.

In marketing, your most valuable business asset is the size and quality of your house mailing list. These are existing customers, or past customers, who have put their hand up as being interested in something you are selling (prospects).

This mailing list is a gold mine—*your* gold mine, to be precise.

If your marketing has done a good job of building relationships with your list, then you have at your disposal an audience of highly engaged customers and prospective customers who will sift and sort themselves along your sales continuum, buying new, better products and services as you move them along that funnel.

John Lennon and Paul McCartney understood this very well. At the time, Paul said, "John would be getting an extension on his house or something, and the joke used to be, 'Okay! Today, let's write a swimming pool.'" Meaning, he understood the value of having a fan base—an audience that would eagerly purchase whatever he was selling—the next song or album, or concert.

So before we start building your marketing engine, you need to understand that the quality and quantity of your mailing list is your gold. I say quality, meaning how engaged and responsive they are. A bigger list is not always better. You can make a lot of money having just a small, highly responsive list of a thousand prospects versus a hundred thousand non-engaged ones.

Pro Secrets to Managing Your Mailing Lists

1. Every name in your database is extremely valuable. Handle with care. Don't delegate this to a junior staff member who doesn't appreciate how valuable this asset is. Just like your checkbook, it needs your eagle eyes to be on it at all times.

2. Every person you or any of your team speak to should also go into your database (with their permission of course).

3. Monitor the size and responsiveness of your mailing list.

4. If you have a crummy CMS (Content Management System)—one that's outdated, unused, non-existent, hard to use—then switch. You don't need fancy. You just need functional. Start with a simple email platform like MailChimp, and you can grow from there.

5. Email addresses are highly valuable. Postal addresses are the next level up, and telephone numbers round out the trifecta of essential info.

6. The more sophisticated your marketing gets, the more you will slice, dice, categorize and tag your customer database to accurately reflect their previous purchases, buyer behaviors, and personal preferences, because the more tailored you can make your marketing message to each of your customers, the higher the response rate. This is a much more advanced level of Client Stampede marketing, but it's good for you to keep in mind as you grow your list.

FUNDAMENTAL TWO: Keep the 3-Legged Stool in Mind Every Time You Advertise.

For a marketing promotion of any kind to work like gangbusters, three things have to match:

1. Your Target Market
2. Your Message
3. Your Media

One of my marketing mentors, Dan Kennedy, called this the three-legged stool of marketing, because if any one of these is mismatched, the stool falls over and your advertising flops.

Conversely, for any marketing that has not yielded great results for you so far, now you know why. Because one, two, or even all three of these were out of alignment.

We've covered Target Market in Step 1, so you know all about the importance of being targeted, and identifying, ideally, rich, deep niches. We've covered Irresistible Messaging in Step 2, so you know the importance of using the right message to resonate with your target market. You've created a list of irresistible offers (matching bait to critter, another Dan Kennedy-ism).

Now you're ready to move on to Media.

Which Media Should You Be Advertising In?

The selection of media can be overwhelming; there are literally thousands of different channels for you to advertise your business on.

Until that is, you narrow it down by studying your target market's buying behavior and social habits. That's when the smoke clears, and you no longer have to fall victim to advertising on the latest marketing fad.

Don't be swayed by what others are doing.

What Will YOUR Marketing Engine Look Like?

ASSEMBLING YOUR MARKETING SYSTEM (ENGINE)

Let's break it down and start with your website—the single most important foundational component of your entire marketing engine.

At the very least, your website needs to make you feel proud when you look at it, be easy to navigate, load quickly (on all browsers and especially on mobile) and convey in five seconds or less what your business does, and how you're better and different. It's your number one branding tool that either convinces a prospect that you're worthy of their time and attention, or not. If your website was built more than three years ago, chances are it's dated and overdue for a total refresh.

Other critical areas your website needs to check off:

- Be easy to navigate—can someone find what they're looking for in two mouse clicks or less?
- A modern feel—no clunky graphics that don't load properly or look sub-par, nice white space on each page to breath.
- Clear calls to action—what do you want visitors to do when they visit? Look around? Call you? Download something helpful?
- Concise, friendly copy that doesn't need a PhD to understand. If people can't understand it, they won't buy.

Don't get tripped up at this basic step. A simple and modern website will outperform a dated and complex website any day.

Now let's move onto your client attraction tools—the advertising you use to attract new leads.

PART 1: YOUR CLIENT ATTRACTION TOOLS

There are literally thousands of different client attraction tools you can use in your marketing engine. As the number of avenues through which we can advertise explodes, so too does the number of possible marketing tools you can use. Don't be overwhelmed by your options.

The great thing about having a marketing system is that as soon as you have its core client attraction tools built and working, you can just adapt what you have for new advertising platforms. No need to reinvent the wheel. But the more lead generation tools you can have working for your business, the stronger your marketing engine. Everyone is looking for that one elusive silver marketing bullet to generate, say, a hundred quality leads. The reality is, it is never one marketing tool that will bring in 100 leads, it's far more likely to be twenty tools that each bring in five quality leads.

Regardless of how many tools you have working for you, every lead generation method needs to be measured and monitored in order to assess performance, and be continually improved.

Here are some of the most commonly used tools, and some pro tips to get the most ROI out of them.

Press articles

Choose a catchy headline that will grab your prospect's attention, then at the end of the article, send them to your website to download something of value.

Billboards

Invest in billboard media that is lit up at night, so your message can be read 24/7. Keep your message and your call to action simple. Use bright, bold colors to grab attention. Don't just invest in single billboards; repetition is key with this media—the more you can invest, the better—as long as they're well placed and highly visible to your target audience.

Blog

Every website needs a blog to help it stay relevant in Google rankings, and to build a relationship with your prospects and customers by sharing helpful information. The more frequently you can post blogs, the better. But don't sacrifice quality for quantity.

Book

These are one of the best expert positioning tools you can have. Make sure the title is something that would stop your target audience in their tracks. Refer to page 81 for more options on how to achieve this.

Educational Video Series

There are so many different ways an educational video series can be used, on your website, or as part of a social media campaign, or as part of your email autoresponders to send to unconverted leads, for example. The video series can be animated, and doesn't have to be shot with actual live footage. Just keep the pace fast, and the content high quality and interesting. No, it doesn't have to be thirty seconds, and yes people do still watch hour-long promotional videos—although, of course, they might think they are watching a documentary or some kind of infotainment instead!

eMagazine or eNewsletter

This is a great tool for building relationships, with prospects and can be sent weekly or monthly. They usually include articles of interest, blogs, maybe something humorous, and any special promotions. It is a very powerful sales tool when used correctly!

Shameless plug alert below!

 Join my weekly eMagazine called Marketing Gold, delivered every Monday to your inbox by visiting **www.ClientStampede.com** and signing up with your best email. It's packed with the best tools, tips and strategies from the trenches (based on marketing that actually works, not theory about what *should* work.)

Social Media Paid Advertising Campaigns

Test lots of different imagery with your ad campaigns and always include a "wildcard" image. You would be surprised at how many times the wildcard image can end up getting the most clicks. Combine your paid advertising strategies with your organic community-building posts. Look to see who your big referrers and brand champions are. Develop those relationships.

Free Special Reports

As we've already discussed, education-based marketing generates the best kind of prospects. Use as many of these in your marketing as you can. Test different headlines.

Google Pay-Per-Click Advertising

Don't even attempt to do this yourself if you're the DIY type. It's become an extremely technical platform, and can be a way to blow a lot of money fast, with little or no results if you don't know what you're doing. If this tool makes sense for your business, shoot us an email, and we can refer you to an agency we trust.

Podcast

This is one of the fastest-growing areas of marketing, and provides a great way for people to get familiar with your business, your brand and to build trust in you. Don't just do one or two episodes. Start with a minimum of ten and build from there. Episodes don't have to be long. I once subscribed to a podcast that gave me a "thought for the day"—it was less than a minute every day.

Press Releases

New innovations, new product and service launches, new key collaborations, new sponsorships, partnerships, book deals, charity support, and expert commentary on current events, all make for excellent press releases. Use the strongest headline possible. Remember, it needs to be written with your target audience in mind and what's of most interest to them. Do not use them as a pat on the back. Consider local, national, and international press release syndication to reach a much wider audience and get the SEO benefit (see below). Services like PRNewswire do a good job of this.

Public Speaking

Have two to three different topics you can talk about—all being of immense interest to your target audience. Have photos taken to use in social media and, where possible, have recordings made. You can even replay this back as part of a website download or giveaway.

Radio

Keep your ads crisp and clear, and use an interesting (signature) jingle at the beginning and end, to build brand identity. Have a simple call to action. Don't get tempted to try gimmicks such as voice talent talking with funny, thick accents, that no-one can understand.

Referrals

Identify your top referrers and find new and better ways to support them, and recognize them, as permitted by law. (However, if you're in the healthcare business, this area is a minefield, so be very careful.) Consider doing co-marketing ad campaigns with other similar companies to increase your referral rates.

SEO

SEO stands for Search Engine Optimization. That's geek-speak for how much Google likes your website and the likelihood of it being ranked on the first page. SEO is driven by a complex, changing algorithm determined by keywords (which is why blogs are so important on your website), the popularity of your articles, how long visitors spend on your website, and an infinite number of other factors. The upshot is, you want very strong SEO, so your target market can easily find your website.

Trade Shows

There's a huge opportunity to do pre-trade show marketing to attendees and post tradeshow marketing. Don't just focus on the actual show itself. The most successful booths provide visitors with an experience—something they seek out and bring others to come experience with them. Don't make the mistake of turning your booth into a hard-sell environment. The goal is to open conversations, make connections, offer value, and build relationships that can happen in minutes, or over days, weeks, or months, depending on the buyer.

Webinars

These are highly valuable lead generation tools, and can be a great leverage of time. They can be easily automated even though they deliver an experience of playing live. Or they can really be live, giving the audience a chance to participate and engage through commenting and asking questions. Sometimes the goal of a webinar is to make a sale. Other times it's to collect an email address and build a relationship by delivering high value first. Be clear on your goals and make your offer irresistible.

PART 2:
YOUR CONVERSION TOOLS

Conversion is the process your company uses to turn a prospect into a paying customer. Sometimes, this might be done entirely digitally (e.g. think of purchasing a product online).

Other conversions may take place on the phone, or in-person at your office. Sometimes it's a one-step click-and-buy process; other times it can involve a complex series of steps that involve many months and many people. Whatever your conversion process, the way to increase your conversion rate is by systemizing, using best practices, and loading the odds in your favor. This is done by having your lead generation marketing answer as many sales objections as possible, before they even reach this step. That way, by the time your leads arrive with their purchase orders or credit cards, they're about 90% certain they'll move forward. All they need is some verification. No selling is needed.

Here are some common examples of conversion tools. Your business might use some, or none, of these. It's important you identify every step in your conversion process, in order to systematize it and maximize its potential.

Sales Scripting

Whether in person or by phone, there's a reason why the world's top sales people use scripts: they work. Even your receptionists who speak to clients and answer phones should be answering questions from a script.

The Money Room

Perhaps your sales discussions take place in a specific room in your office. One of our financial advisory service clients calls this their "money room." What does it look like? Is it a room that is welcoming, that someone would want to hang out in? Or is it cluttered with battered furniture and old files? Does it feel so cold and inviting that someone might want to escape as soon as possible? And what's the actual sales process like? Do you get your clients to handwrite and complete endless pieces of paper, or is everything digitized and made as simple and as seamless as possible?

Digital Sales Experience

If you're transacting sales online, you need to micromanage every single step of the process. Is the shopping cart experience easy to navigate? How many clicks does it take to check out? Do you have an abandoned cart email campaign that triggers if someone doesn't finish the transaction? What kind of thank you message do you offer? If you have a new client, how do you welcome them to your business? What kind of follow-up is there? How easy is it for them to contact the service desk and speak to an actual person? If there's an issue, how easily and quickly can it be resolved? What's your review process like? And so on.

Shock n' Awe Package

This is a great tool to add to your marketing system when you're selling high-value products and services, or if you have a sales process that can take weeks or months. A Shock n' Awe package is sent to a prospect early on in the conversion process, to welcome them to your business, impress them with your track record and share valuable information to help them make a better decision. Typically, these are physically mailed packages (digital packages aren't anywhere near as effective), and should showcase your brand at every touchpoint—from the box it's mailed in, to the quality of the contents, to the phone call follow-up afterwards.

PART 3: YOUR CLIENT RETENTION TOOLS

The secret with retention marketing is to make it as personalized as possible. You want your customers to feel loved and special, so the more customized you can make your marketing to them, the better. For example, create special offers that are ONLY available to existing clients. Who does this? Usually, a special offer is only available to a new client!

Here are a few examples and tips to get you started:

Email Campaigns

Email will quickly become the MVP (most valuable player) of your marketing engine, if it isn't already. The eMagazine or eNewsletter that you use for client attraction can be used as a retention tool also, either by simply sending it to everyone on your email list, or creating a separate issue for your clients only. Other email campaigns can be sent with tailored offers based on a client's specific interests and past purchasing history. This is an area of huge, usually very untapped, opportunity!

Celebration Campaigns

Client anniversaries, children's graduations, birthdays—these are events special to your client that your company can celebrate by way of a special offer. A card in the mail goes a very long way, but an email does too if that's not possible.

Direct Mail

Contrary to what you may have been led to believe, direct mail is not dead. That's why Google uses it regularly as part of their Marketing engine (I personally get a postcard in the mail from Google at least every two months). Putting together a special direct mail campaign takes effort and investment, but the returns can be exceptional. Your clients will also appreciate your business taking the extra step of doing this, instead of just shooting off an email, especially if your target market is people aged 55 and older.

Client Only Events, Seminars and Webinars

Make being a client of your company mean something. Create exclusive access. Help your clients solve their problems by showing them that your new products, or existing services, are the solution, and move them up the ascension ladder.

 ### Not Always a Slam Dunk. Marketing Is about the Pivot.

Do we create marketing campaigns that are always a home run? No. *I wish.* That would be *some* super power. But we do know the next best thing—how to load the dice in our client's favor, by having insight on what's worked the best in the past, what the major pain points are, and some of the best ways to capture and keep customers' attention by strategic positioning and great advertising.

The key thing about marketing is the ability to pivot when you see something is not working. Maybe your offer wasn't irresistible enough? Maybe your ads are not targeting the right audience? Maybe there's an issue with your website that is preventing people from checking out and making a purchase. Maybe your headline needs work. When a marketing campaign doesn't work, it doesn't necessarily mean it's a dud. It could mean it's incredibly powerful and needs one or two tiny things to be tweaked. I've seen many, many examples of campaigns that were not performing, but with little changes made here and there, they've turned into big winners. Thanks to digital marketing, you don't have to bet the farm on a new campaign. You can start out by testing new messages, new offers, new ad creative using micro budgets, and get almost instant feedback on its success.

 Got a campaign that's not working? Download our FREE Advertising Campaign Critique Tool to help troubleshoot the problem by visiting **www.ClientStampedeBook.com**

Bravo! Now you've assembled your marketing engine. It's ready to run. But don't forget your *marketing gas!*

Let's Talk about the Difference: Marketing Engine vs Marketing Gas

Your Marketing Engine is your marketing *system* which is comprised of mostly evergreen marketing tools, sales systems and procedures, which are used again and again.

The bigger your marketing engine—meaning the more marketing tools you have in place—the faster your organization can grow. Investing in a marketing engine is like investing in machinery, or a new technology platform for your company.

However, in order for an engine to run, it also needs Marketing Gas. In marketing terms, **your marketing gas is the marketing**

budget that you invest every month to keep your marketing engine running. This is your disposable marketing cost.

All your third-party media costs are your marketing gas, but the creation of the marketing pieces themselves are your marketing engine.

For example:

MARKETING ENGINE	MARKETING GAS
	All the monthly marketing attraction tools designed to bring quality traffic (eyeballs) to your website eg monthly blog posts, SEO, etc
Your Website (your online store/digital office HQ)	
Facebook Advertising Campaign: images, ad copy, irresistible offer, landing page	Media spend on Facebook per month or per campaign
Billboard Campaign: Billboard ad design(s), call to action, special offer	Media spend paid to billboard company, charged per billboard per month
Radio Ad campaign: Scripting and recording of 30 and 60-second radio ads, creation of irresistible offer, special landing page on website	Media spend to radio company charged on number of ad airings, endorsement by radio host

In other words, *Marketing Gas* is your monthly advertising budget. It's a disposable cost. Your *Marketing Engine* on the other hand, is the machine that runs all your advertising and maximizes every dollar of your marketing budget.

Most companies don't understand the difference. They invest their money in marketing gas every month but have no marketing engine to maximize, or even manage results. So they waste enormous amounts of dollars throwing money into marketing platforms, hoping something works.

The good news is that if you have a properly built marketing engine, then you need less gas to run it, because there aren't leaks in the gas tank. By that I mean every unconverted lead gets added to your marketing system. Your new and old client relationships are being maximized and strengthened. Every "drop of gas" is being optimized. **Just like an accelerator pedal, you can add more or less gas into your engine, depending on your needs.**

How Much Marketing Gas Does Your Company Need?

The lame, default answer is: well, that depends. How competitive is your industry? How ambitious are your growth goals? What's your annual revenue? What's your projected annual revenue? How strong is your marketing engine, blah blah blah. All of these are key variables in answering that rather loaded question. We've worked with clients on a turbo timeframe with big goals who invested 27% of their target revenue on marketing gas. Still others might be around the 7% of revenue model. The average, if there is such a thing, is around 10% of revenue.

Well hold up! Not sure what to include in your Marketing Engine? Get more help by downloading The Client Stampede Business Blueprint™. It's awesome and it's FREE. Visit **www.ClientStampedeBook.com** to grab it.

We have one more step. The icing on the cake: Extraordinary experience.

"Nothing in this world can take the place of persistence. Talent will not: nothing is more common than unsuccessful men with talent. Genius will not; unrewarded genius is almost a proverb. Education will not: the world is full of educated derelicts. Persistence and determination alone are omnipotent"

CALVIN COOLIDGE

STEP 7

Extraordinary Experience

Creating Extraordinary Experience

"There is always room at the top."

- DANIEL WEBSTER

magine this scenario for a minute. It's 6pm, and you're already running late to get home to change and go to dinner. But first, you have to grab some groceries because, of course, there's no ɔod for Fido, and you're out of all your everyday essentials, like ɔolombian espresso coffee, and your favorite Pinot Noir. As you wing into the grocery car park, the heavens open, and a deluge of ain pelts your car. It's not letting up. So you bravely throw open ɪe door, making a mad dash for the entrance. You've got no coat nd no umbrella. Looking like a drowned rat, you push your cart uickly around the store throwing in items left and right. You check ut. The cashier looks at you pitifully, as the puddles gather around our feet. Still, the rain hasn't let up. If anything, it has intensified. Jow you have to get a whole cart of groceries to your car as well as ourself without drowning.

Given how tired, wet, and irritable you are, which of these would constitute an extraordinary experience?

1) If the cashier handed you a big (branded) umbrella and said, "here, use this and keep it in your car for next time, thanks for shopping with us."

2) If the cashier called up their concierge valet to go get your car, park it out front, and load all your groceries for you while you watched, happily eating freshly baked cookies and drinking espresso. Or a glass of Cabernet.

3) If you never actually had to leave your car in the first place. As you pulled in and the heavens opened, you dialed and requested a personal shopper who was immediately available to walk the aisles swiftly, providing live video footage of the fresh produce, as you directed them to what to buy. Checkout was via a link sent to your phone. The groceries were promptly brought to your car and loaded in carefully while you caught up on your latest favorite episode.

Would any of these experiences be rave-worthy to you? Enough to tell your spouse or your friends or to post about on social media?

This final step of the Client Stampede Formula™ is optional but highly recommended.

And it's a FREE source of marketing gas for your marketing engine (word of mouth marketing) and another competitive advantage. Sadly, it doesn't take much these days for your business to be considered extraordinary, because the general standards are so low.

Here are some examples of **Extraordinary Experiences that are really not so extraordinary, that also fit the definition:**

A medical practice with a No-More-Than-5-Minute-Wait Guarantee. If you're sitting in the waiting room for longer than ten minutes, you get a $20 Starbucks gift voucher. Seriously, which medical practice has enough guts to implement this policy? It would blow up social media. And it would dramatically increase the operational efficiency of a medical practice.

The plumber/contractor/electrician/tradesperson who, after he works in your house or office, cleans up after themselves so there is NO TRACE and even runs a vacuum or mop over the surrounding area so that it's actually cleaner than before work started. This happened to me once. I was dumbfounded. I must have told at least fifty people and I have written about it multiple times since.

The pediatric dentist who has a "kids lab" and lets them make their own toothpaste, which they get to take home and use with their new personalized toothbrush kit.

The SAAS company who doesn't just do everything digitally. They mail their customers a cool "welcome to the family" kit that includes t-shirts, mugs, and mousepads, and sends birthday presents to their customers.

The online pet store that sends their customers greeting cards on their pet's birthday along with a free hand-painted portrait, and flowers when they pass away.

Here are some more examples of companies who have created an Extraordinary Experience:

Jet Blue's Surprise Caffeine Fix

A man named Paul Brown was flying JetBlue airlines when he casually tweeted that he couldn't grab his Starbucks coffee before boarding the plane because he was flying out of the smaller terminal at Boston's Logan airport. Within seconds of seeing the tweet, the JetBlue staff sprang into action and organized for the airport customer service representative to deliver a Starbucks "venti mocha" to his seat on the plane before take off. As you can imagine Paul was elated and tweeted about the experience which went viral.

Tesla's Mobile Mechanic

Tesla has removed the aggravation of having to take your car to the dealership by bringing their own mobile mechanic van to an owner's home. A customer called Chris Kern tweeted this: *Flat tire on Sunday. Called Tesla, [got] a loaner tire within 40 minutes. Today they came to my house to replace the tire in 10 minutes. scheduled to come back to fix a small issue next week. What other car company does this?*

Trader Joe's To The Rescue

An 89-year-old man was stuck in his house during a snowstorm and his daughter was worried he wouldn't have enough food. She called around to several grocery stores and asked if they would deliver, but no one would brave the storm. Finally, Trader Joe's said they normally didn't deliver, but they'd be happy to help. The daughter read off a long list of items to the store and the staff then made some helpful suggestions of products they might want to add since her Dad was on a low-sodium diet. At the conclusion of the call, the store refused payment and delivered the entire order within 30 minutes, all free of charge.

The Ritz-Calton's Daily Catch and
The Missing Giraffe

A customer at the Ritz Carlton in Boston had caught a large tuna (200 lbs) on a fishing trip during his stay. He told the doorman that the fish was in the cooler in the car, and asked if he could have some more ice for the cooler. Going above and beyond what was asked, the doorman asked the kitchen supervisor to clean the fish and break it down into smaller pieces for the guest. Then, the supervisor cleaned the cooler, and arranged the pieces of tuna in fresh ice so that they would be ready to cook or freeze when the customer returned home.

When a little boy realized he had left his beloved stuffed giraffe behind at the Ritz-Carlton in Amelia Island, FL, he was beside himself. His dad told his tearful son that Joshie was just taking an extra few days of vacation at the hotel and would be back soon. The dad called the hotel and was relieved to learn that they had Joshie, so he asked if they would help him substantiate his "vacation" story by taking a picture of Joshie relaxing by the pool to send with him. The team at the Ritz-Carlton did more than that. They took pictures of Joshie all over the hotel – getting a massage at the spa, driving a golf cart, and making new friends. They packaged all the photos up in a book, and sent them along with Josie the giraffe, to a very happy little boy (and relieved Dad).

Here's the acid test of an Extraordinary Experience: "Would this give our customers bragging rights and/or surprise and delight them?"

What could you implement in your company that would give your customers bragging rights?

"You don't need luck. You are powerful, clever, and fearless."

SHANNON HALE

(Not) Final Words

"It doesn't matter if the glass is half-full, or half-empty. All that matters is that you are the one pouring the water."

MARK CUBAN

"Remember this, dear, if you play small, you stay small."

UNKNOWN

A huge congratulations, you've reached the end of the book!

Your Client Stampede journey begins today!

1. What are the top three things you've learned from this book that you can go away and implement immediately in your business?

2. Of all seven steps, which one do you think represents the greatest area of weakness in your business, which, by addressing it, can be turned into one of your greatest areas of strength?

Your business is extraordinary. You are extraordinary. The world needs your business to be extremely successful, to serve and inspire others and make the world a better place.

As we say in New Zealand, "Go get 'em!"

"Never, never, never give up"

WINSTON CHURCHILL

Common Marketing Problems, and Their Solutions

We Get a Poor Response to Digital Marketing

Our company does a ton of digital advertising on a lot of different platforms, but we're not getting the response we used to. Why is this?

Solution

There can be many reasons why your response rate is declining. Here are some of the most common reasons:

- Your target audience has shifted away from the platforms you're advertising on

- Your brand is fatigued—people have become numb to your imagery and messaging

- Your offer isn't irresistible enough

- There might be a technical reason—perhaps the platforms are actually not showing your campaigns as much as they used to, or your target audience is off

- There might be an unknown issue with something in your campaign that's preventing people from responding, e.g. the links you are sending people to are broken, the landing page is dull or difficult to understand, the download has stopped working, the ecommerce checkout is too cumbersome.

We Have a Lot of Website Traffic but Low Conversions

I have a lot of traffic coming to my website but no one is buying anything, or calling me, or filling out a contact form? Why is no one doing anything? What can I do to fix it?

Solution

There are likely two main reasons for this:

1) either the traffic you're attracting is low quality and not truly your target market, and/or;

2) your website might need an overhaul or tune up because it's preventing people from taking the action you want.

I recommend you go back to Step 1 of the Client Stampede Formula™ and make sure you're targeting the right people first. Then take a close look at your website and the experience of your visitors, as well as the various calls to action you are using on your website. Are the actions clear and easy to do? Are you providing your visitors with a great first impression, or are things cluttered and not visually appealing? Remember that not all traffic is created equal!

Help, We Have a Large Social Media Following Who Doesn't Buy

We have a large social media following. We post, tweet, comment and share regularly, but we don't seem get much new business. Why is this?

Solution

First, check Step 1 of The Client Stampede Formula™, your target market. Make sure they truly are on social media, and are on the platforms you're active on.

Then move to Step 2 and look at your messaging. Does it resonate with your target audience? Are you seeking to serve, educate and be of genuine help? Or are you too salesy and putting people off? Consider reaching out to some of your community who are active and ask them what you can do to improve. Their feedback will be invaluable.

We Rebranded but It Hasn't Grown Business

We just invested a lot of money to rebrand our business. The feedback has been positive but we haven't noticed any difference to our sales volumes.

Solution

This may be because your rebrand was more of a band-aid type of approach, and gave you a new logo and color scheme, but wasn't a truly top-down rebrand that actually *repositioned your business and conveyed a higher level of value to your customers.* Sorry to be blunt but you can't put lipstick on a pig.

Getting a new logo and a new website isn't truly a rebrand. It's lipstick. You need to apply Step 3 of the Client Stampede Formula™ (having already done Step 1 and 2). This will get you further, faster, but remember, if you're truly looking to transform your business, Power Branding is just one component. You'll need to apply all 7 steps of the Client Stampede Formula™ to truly transform your business.

If you need more help, check out the Client Stampede Ultimate Marketing Toolkit and Fast Start Training on **www.ClientStampede.com**

We Have Wildly Fluctuating Cashflow

My revenue lurches from feast to famine. Sometimes I am so busy and can't catch my breath. Other times it's extremely quiet. How can I fix this?

Solution

Don't worry, this is one of the most common marketing problems! Read Step 6 on Building Your Marketing Engine. Consistent, effective marketing is key to ironing out all your slow periods, and puts you in control of when you attract new business (not the other way around)!

We Want to Raise Prices Without Losing Customers

We want to raise prices but we're already at the high end of what we can charge, and have enough customers complaining. How can we raise our prices without losing business?

Solution

I'm so glad you asked! See the case study and walk-through example I discussed in Step 5 on Pricing.

We Are Using Traditional Marketing like Direct Mail but We Want Bigger Results

We started using direct mail again in our business (like Google does) and we're getting good results, but we want higher conversion rates. What ideas have you got?

Solution

Oh, so many ideas! First of all, who are you mailing to? Where are you buying your lists from? Are you using lumpy mail? How personalized are your direct mail campaigns? How irresistible are your offers? How are you integrating your direct mail campaigns with your digital marketing efforts (especially your website)? It sounds like you are at an advanced level of marketing and might be ready for one of our mastermind programs. Visit clientstampede. com to learn more.

Help! Our Competitors Keep Undercutting Our Prices

We are in a cut-throat marketplace and our sales volume keeps decreasing month after month. We're getting undercut by our competitors. What do you advise?

Hmm, sounds like your marketing strategy is all based around price instead of value. Step 5 of the Client Stampede Formula™ on pricing will definitely be an eye-opener in terms of how you can transform this.

I Am Overwhelmed. Where Do I Start?

What should I be doing to get the most bang for my marketing bucks?

Solution

The fact you've bought this book and have read this far already puts you ahead of 95% of the competitors in your market, so BRAVO!

Step 1 – make sure you downloaded the free marketing tools at **www.ClientStampedeBook.com** Go through each of these three documents and see what insights you can glean for your business. Can you use the advertising checklist? What a-ha moments did you get from working through the mini business blueprint? Now it's time to implement.

Step 2 – Choose just one key action to implement in your own business from this book – just one and put it into action *today*.

Step 3 – Subscribe to The Client Stampede Podcast on your favorite podcast channel and start with the first episode. You don't need to listen in order but the first episode is a good place to start.

"A ship is safe in harbor, but that's not what ships are for."

WILLIAM G.T. SHEDD

About Julie Guest

Julie Guest is a bestselling author, popular speaker and trusted marketing advisor to private clients across the globe running businesses from $1 Million to $1 Billion+. She is the CEO of Bolder&Louder, a full-service marketing agency that specializes in branding and transformational marketing; uncovering hidden opportunities, creating new opportunities, repositioning products and re-inventing businesses.

Julie is the founder of the Client Stampede Marketing School and Coaching Company—serving busy entrepreneurs who refuse to follow the herd, and whose businesses make the world better. Julie is regularly featured in various media, including Forbes, the New York Times, USA Today, Entrepreneur magazine, and many others.

When she's not helping others build a bigger, better business, you can usually find her riding one of her horses, spending time with her family, or doing a bucket-list travel adventure to some far-flung corner of the world.

You can connect with Julie on LinkedIn or on Facebook @clientstampede

Visit **www.ClientStampede.com** or **www.BolderLouder.com** or **www.LunchBreakBooks.com** for more information.

SHORT ON TIME?
HERE ARE THE CLIFF NOTES

1. There's a Grand Canyon sized difference between marketing strategy and marketing tactics. You DON'T need more marketing tactics to attract tons of new clients (what everyone would have you believe). You just need better strategy.

2. When every one else in your market is going left, bank right.

3. Don't believe them when they tell you "it" can't be done. It can be done and will work out far better than "they" could imagine.

4. You need a marketing engine yesterday – it will become your most valuable business asset, will solve all your marketing problems and will deliver unbelievable ROI. Make it your top priority.

5. Have more fun – especially with your marketing. We all need to laugh more. Your customers and your staff will thank you for it.

GET STARTED NOW BY DOWNLOADING YOUR FREE CLIENT STAMPEDE BUSINESS BLUEPRINT™, TRAINING AND MARKETING TOOLS

Visit www.ClientStampedeBook.com

SUBSCRIBE TO
THE CLIENT STAMPEDE
PODCAST

**Don't miss an episode.
Subscribe today on iTunes or
your favorite podcast channel.**

THE CLIENT STAMPEDE

MARKETING SCHOOL &
PODCAST

Popular Episodes:

Episode #1 There Is No Power In Playing Small

Episode #17 Oops Are You Doing Tactic Marketing?

Episode #20 SALE! Why This Could Be The Worst Strategy For Your Business

Episode #41 You're So Much Better Than Your Competitors. It's Time More People Realized That.

DISCOVER HOW TO AUTHOR YOUR MOST POWERFUL MARKETING ASSET ON YOUR LUNCH BREAK — AND HAVE YOUR DREAM CLIENTS READ IT ON THEIRS.

Here's How To Write And Publish A Book That Positions YOU As The Expert In Just 60 Minutes...

Most people think that writing a book takes months of hard work, slogging it out in a room on your own.

Discover the quicker, easier way to become a published author and get your book outlined, written and published in as much time as it takes to eat your lunch.

Download your free copy today by visiting **www.LunchBreakBooks.com**

Acknowledgments

There are so many people I'd like to thank, who have helped me on this incredible journey.

First, a big thank you to my family for always being there for me, even when I've chosen to live on a different continent and do things "the hard way". Yes, Dale, you were right, the black sheep of the family! I love you all.

A huge thank you to my angel Marilyn and all the family for your amazing support in helping me raise my little one—I could not have done any of this without you (… by the grace of God).

Thank you to my own amazing team. You are exceptional and I'm so grateful to each and every one of you for your incredible contributions to our clients. And a huge thank you to Josie especially, for all the small and big things you do every day to make my life easier and our businesses run more smoothly.

Thank you to all our clients and coaching students. Because of you, I get to do what I love to do the most, every single day. My brain is hard wired for helping you strategically build your businesses. It's an honor and a privilege to serve you.

A huge thank you to Miranda and Nush, for always being there—the late night texts, video chats and, of course, our decades of many incredible adventures together. And a big thank you to Tony, my amazing friend and marketing wingman – ten years and counting!

And thank you to all my marketing, business and life mentors who have coached me, inspired me, and helped me along the way, including Robert Cialdini, Dan Kennedy, Gary Halbert, David Ogilvy, Gary Benzivenga, Dan Sullivan, Kathy Kolbe, Christine Kane, Kathy Ireland, Og Mandino, Paul Arden, Hiro Boga, Tosha Silver, Tim Ferriss, Charlie Mackesy, Maya Angelou, Florence Shinn, Jeffrey Gitomer, Robert Ringer, Gary Vee, Noah Kagan, Keith Ferrazzi, Robert Cialdini and Rich Schefren.

Thank you to my editors, Jon and Victoria, to Lili and all my team at Blue Sky Publishing, and to Ivan The Great for creating such a kick-butt cover (and sticking with me through fifty plus variations LOL!).

From the bottom of my heart, I appreciate you all.

"If they say
it's impossible, it's
impossible for them
not for you."

MUHAMMAD ALI

"I am not afraid. I was born to do this."

JOAN OF ARC

"Give light and people will find a way."

ELLA BARKER

ONE ASK

Did you learn anything valuable from reading The Client Stampede? If so, I'd be very grateful if you could help me build my client stampede by taking action and doing any of the following:

1. Give this book a five-star review on your favorite online retailer. Every review goes a long way!
2. Let's connect on Facebook @clientstampede
3. Connect with me on LinkedIn @JulieGuest
4. Subscribe to the Client Stampede podcast on your favorite podcast platform

THANK YOU!

Lightning Source UK Ltd.
Milton Keynes UK
UKHW020640161121
394011UK00007B/495